THE LONG ROAD TO PEACE

To Jim,
in friendship,

matthew

THE LONG ROAD TO PEACE

Encounters with the People of Southern Sudan

MATHEW HAUMANN MHM

First published in 2000

Gracewing
2 Southern Avenue, Leominster
Herefordshire HR6 0QF

ISBN 0 85244 520 2

Typeset by Action Publishing Technology Ltd,
Gloucester GL1 1SP

Printed by MPG Books Ltd,
Bodmin PL31 1EG

CONTENTS

PREFACE AND DEDICATION

I am dark and beautiful
Daughters of Jerusalem.
Do not remark that my skin is dark,
Darkened by the sun.
The sons of my mother disliked me,
Made me to work in their vineyards.
My own vineyard – I could not care for.

The Song of Songs 1.5–6.

Far from our world, somewhere in the Upper Nile
Province of Sudan, he sat reading by the great river. In my
baggage he had found a book about the history of
Christianity in Africa, and there was the passage from the
Song of Songs. He checked it against the Bible that he had
carried with him since his return from Ethiopia a few
years ago.

He spoke to me about it in the evening. To him it is
clear that this text speaks of himself and his people. Like
many Sudanese, he feels at home with the stories of the
Bible, especially the Old Testament. He assured me that
his country was here in the time of the Song of Songs and
that the journey of his people with God had endured
much longer than the couple of hundred years since
Christianity came to the land. Indeed here Christianity
was older than the two thousand years of Christendom. I
had to laugh at that, but later I realized the truth of what
he said, for the Old Testament *is* undeniably part of the
history of Christianity.

It was as if this Nuer catechist wanted to put me at ease,
telling me that I was in God's own country and that I did
not have to worry. I thought of how Jung in 1925, on his
only visit to Africa, was told, 'You know, mister, this here

is not man's country, it is God's country. So, if anything happens, just sit down and don't worry.'[1] For centuries, the Sudanese have been exploited and oppressed by the white people and by the Arabs. But this catechist, and many with him, is convinced that the day will come when their land will stand among the nations, strong and free.

I have witnessed the humiliation and exploitation of the people in the south, and how the fundamentalist Islamic government works to enslave them. A mountain of reports has been written about Sudan: political analysis, the relief programmes, human rights violations, and so on. These reports contain the woeful statistics; they have their own value and usually are better documented than the stories in this book. It is good to remember that these reports are ultimately about people. Here, I have often met these people, men and women who are proud and free despite, or perhaps because of, the long war and fight for freedom. I am glad to have met them and would like to introduce them to you. To these proud and free people I would like to dedicate the stories that follow. These stories are of encounters with people who struggle, each in his or her own way, for freedom. Meeting them has been a liberating experience for me.

These are true stories, not fiction; but where names, circumstances or locations obscured the truth, I have taken the liberty of changing them.

Mathew Haumann

---

[1]Jung, *Memories, Dreams and Reflections*, p. 285.

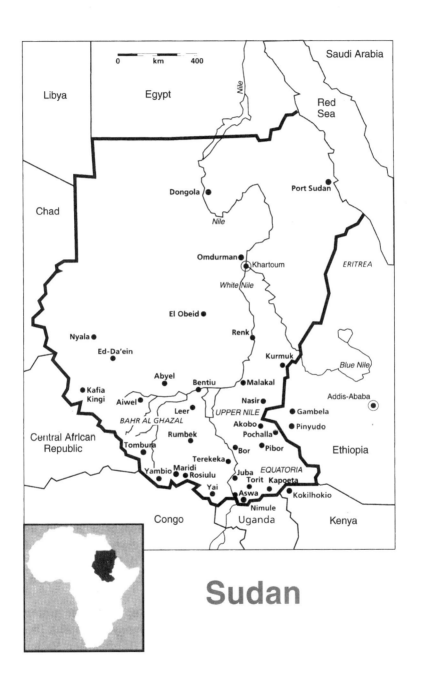

Sudan

MISSION IMPOSSIBLE: POSSIBLY MISSION

Not to know is bad, not to wish to know is worse
Nigerian proverb

When in 1963 I was sent to Africa as a missionary, I was confident that I had a mission there. I had been sent by my own local church, by my own missionary society, to preach 'our' Good News to the young church in Africa. At that time it was understood that the missionary was sent to a 'mission country' to bring the Good News. It was just before the Second Vatican Council ended, and while we were convinced that we possessed the Good News, we did not really suppose Africa could have any good news for us, nor that at times we ourselves might have been bad news. In no way do I want to belittle the work of us missionaries, I want only to highlight some aspects which in the past did not receive much attention.

In 1963, I was convinced that mission belongs to the essence of the Church, I still am. Christ himself told his apostles, 'Peace be with you. As the Father sent me, so I send you' (John 20.21). And elsewhere he tells them, 'Go throughout the whole world and preach the gospel to all people' (Mark 16.15). For me there is no doubt that the Church has a mission nor that the Church *is* mission. We receive that mission when we are baptized, which means that this mission is not the exclusive property of priests and religious who have joined a missionary society, as I have. Every Christian is sent, including all the people whom we have baptized in Africa.

After more than thirty years as a missionary in Africa I

have become confused. On leave in Europe I wonder, 'Who sends me?' It is clear that the church in Europe is currently experiencing uncertainty, and one observes an unspoken fear that we have nothing or very little to give others. Too few of us perceive mission as receiving as much as giving. Especially during the years in Sudan, I often felt the church there was sending me. There have been times that the Sudanese told me, 'Go and tell your people what you have seen'. Mission is not in the first place concerned with the conversion of others, but the conversion of ourselves, the Church (*Ad Gentes* 2). If that is true, then it is also clear that there is mission everywhere, on all continents.

The question is not whether we have a mission, but how we carry out that mission. During my thirty years in Africa the concept of mission has changed. With my pre-Vatican II training, I still went out to convert the pagan, the heathen. Strangely enough, instead of finding pagans I found deeply religious people, and I started to discover the pagan in myself. There have been times when I thought mission was an impossibility. But it is not easy to give up a dream, and I keep hoping that mission is possible after all. Whatever the case, mission cannot only be a one-way street. If we expect other people to be open to our good news, we ourselves must be open to their good news.

This certainly has not always been the case in the European church's interaction with Africa. We hardly believed that Africa had something to say to us. The continent has been open to our good news in spite of the fact that it has been wrapped in western culture, which means at times bad news for Africa. Detractors have dismissed the missionary activity of westerners as cultural imperialism, and I know some Africans who have experienced it as such. Nowadays the church in Africa is talking about 'inculturation', but in the past our approach to mission was more a process of 'deculturation'. In bringing the gospel we often uprooted people from their own culture.

We talk about mission as dialogue, but with Africa we have been hardly on speaking terms. When it comes to the East, there *is* dialogue. The East–West relationship is not one-sided: the Church listens to the mysticism, the spirituality of India and Japan. Zen masters teach us to meditate. We see Oriental spirituality as enriching the Church. In the western hemisphere, the liberation theology born in Latin America is a source of inspiration for many Europeans. Only think of the model of basic Christian communities: even those who disagree with it, will take note. But when you consider Africa, the dialogue has hardly begun. Our relationship with the African peoples has a history of prejudice and mistrust: the missionary often held the same prejudices as the colonialist. Lawrence Nemer, who has studied the attitudes of the Roman Catholic Mill Hill Missionaries and the CMS Missionaries of the Anglican Church in the nineteenth century, indicates how these missionaries saw 'the poor heathen' in Sudan:

> The lamentable condition of this multitude of our fellow creatures, living without the knowledge of God and redemption, living in idolatry, superstition and most abominable sin, and dying miserably in that condition, must excite the compassion of everyone who has a heart to love and feel pity.[1]

It is our prejudices that engender the distrust towards us. I often think that we are the poorer for it, and that is one of the reasons why conflicts between Africa and the West continue.

When we start realizing how poor our churches in the West have become, we might be more open to listen to churches in other parts of the world. In this context I find it interesting that nowadays I not infrequently meet young lay missionaries who will say that they go to Africa to find their faith, rather than to bring it. This does not mean that the Africans necessarily will be open to share their riches when suddenly, after a century of arrogance, we change our attitude. I think that there are times when the Africans are inclined to give up on us. They are well aware of what has happened in the past. In all this, I do not want to say that the missionaries duplicate colonial culture, but in the

---

[1]Quoted from Lawrence Nemer, *Anglican and Roman Catholic Attitudes on Mission*, Steyler Verlag, 1981, p. 150.

past they often had a lot in common with the colonialist. In Kenya there is a saying: *A man who has once been tossed by a buffalo, when he sees a black ox, thinks it another buffalo.*

Some missionaries are inclined to abandon Africa and look for mission elsewhere, and I admit, I too have considered it. I once talked this over with an old African friend in Sudan where, after many decades, the Mill Hill Missionaries have nearly all left. He said, 'When there are problems in a marriage, a divorce is often not the solution. The marriage between Mill Hill and the Church of Malakal is an old one. There has been a time that they were separated from each other. This marriage has been fruitful, but there are problems. After nearly forty years of war, Sudan isn't exactly an attractive bride any more. We in Africa might take a second wife, but that does not mean that we will leave our first wife, the mother of so many children.' This friend certainly sees mission as a partnership where one not only gives but also receives. Africa has its own riches amid its poverty.

Laurens van der Post, who grew up with Africans and was partly raised by an African nanny, often wrote about these African riches. In one of his books he says,

> There is no solution for the conflict in Africa, or in the world, unless there is first of all a change of heart and understanding of man, and I do not see how that change of heart can come about until the white man in Africa starts to think about himself in a new way ... We force the African continually to take from us and prevent him from giving to us in his own rich way; we deny Africa its own unique creativeness.[2]

Laurens van der Post was not writing about missionaries, but I believe that for us his words hold true. Our mission concerns not only the conversion of Africa, but also our own complete change of heart.

Fortunately, during my stay in Africa, in Kenya, Sudan

---

[2]Laurens van der Post, *The Dark Eye in Africa*, New York, Morrow & Company, 1955, pp. 19–25.

and Zaïre, there always have been occasions when a dialogue with Africans came about. Often they were during times when I felt defeated, or when I was willing to let the African lead me. These moments have turned out to be rich ones for me, easing the burden of my heavy baggage. Such dialogue cannot be organized; it just happens spontaneously when people are together in willing receptivity. I have written of some of these encounters because I think they can enrich others just as they have enriched me.

'Sitting under a tree chatting with the natives', is often considered a waste of time by westerners. In Africa people call it *making time*, an African cottage industry. In European culture there are very few people left who know how to make time. The Africans often make time under the tree, for themselves, for each other, but also for the missionary, if he or she is willing to share it. Maybe it is understandable that in the West we have become jealous of our time after being told that it is the equivalent of money. For the greater part of my stay in Africa I made myself continuously busy, running around, always short of time. I was to learn that in war there are times when you can do little; you must sit tight and stay put.

But even during the busy times of peace there were always occasions when the Africans had to slow me down, when they invited me to sit with them under the tree. There, under the tree, dialogue can be born; there together we can discover what mission is really all about. The stories in this book are part of that mission, of being open to the Good News, which Africans and westerners might be for each other.

I am still looking for a good definition of Mission. One that appeals to me more and more is, 'Mission is to sit where the people sit and let God happen'. This definition is not my own invention; I read it somewhere and it stuck because it seems to fit with the African culture. When I shared this definition with an African colleague he commented that this was a very good definition of Mission, provided that we did not think that in this dialogue we also had to speak to God. With a smile he added: 'In Africa, God is old and wise enough to speak for himself and he does not need any lawyers'.

FREEDOM FIGHTER

Poverty is slavery
Somali proverb

I am fairly new in Sudan when I meet John for the first time in 1989 in the market-place of Yambio. This is not his home. Like so many people in Sudan the war has forced him to leave home. John has no idea whether his brothers and sisters are still alive. They live in Kapoeta, Eastern Equatoria. Their original home was somewhere near Juba, but the war has exiled them to Kapoeta, an area in the hands of the Sudan People's Liberation Army. Now it is in the hands of the SPLA but tomorrow it might be in the hands of the government again. John Lakrimoi calls the SPLA freedom fighters; others call them rebels. His brothers and sisters may have been liberated by the SPLA, or may have been killed, John does not know. Western Equatoria, where John and I live, is mainly in the hands of the Sudanese government. The people are very critical of this government, but they are also somewhat afraid of this SPLA. According to SPLA radio this area is 'enemy territory'. They have a broadcast at three o'clock every afternoon, one of the weapons used in this war. The broadcast is almost a sacred hour in southern Sudan: policemen, soldiers, ordinary citizens, they all listen, their ears glued to the radio. John has no radio, and today, as often, he listens with me to my radio in the shade of a tree before my house.

As I listen to the news, I watch how John listens. I guess he is between forty and fifty years old. He looks fit, with well-developed muscles on his arms, like a body-builder. He listens with his whole body, twisting his face in disgust, then shaking his head in disagreement or shrugging his shoulders in doubt, weighing the news and offering his spontaneous commentary as if he is engaged in a lively conversation with the newscaster. His commentary often helps me understand more of this complicated war. Triumphantly the SPLA reports that they have captured Kaya, and are marching on to Yei. They mention the numbers of vehicles and weapons they have seized. The names and ranks of the government soldiers who have been killed are given in detail. Government soldiers who have defected to the SPLA are welcomed elaborately. John is all ears. Granted the SPLA exaggerates, but what they say is rarely a complete fairy tale. Some people here support the SPLA but they do not dare admit it, as they fear the government will penalize them for it. John supports the ideals of the SPLA, though he does not always agree with their methods. But there is nothing secretive about John.

He is critical of both the government and the SPLA. Each has made use of the weapon worse than guns, starvation. Both the SPLA and the government are guilty of blocking food convoys, and hundreds of thousands have died of starvation. And this war goes on and on. For a moment before Christmas it looked like there might be peace. There were peace negotiations in Nairobi, and I had glimpsed hope. I wanted very much to believe that there would be peace; wars wears you out no end. But John Lakrimoi had warned me against such thought: 'Never will there be peace as long as we in the south are treated as *abeed*, as slaves. Even last year many women and children were sold as slaves'. John is convinced that the slave trade still goes on in Sudan, and I believe him. He continues: 'In their eyes I am a slave, but you don't rank very highly either: they call you a "Christian dog".' Given that he has the name of John, one may presume that he had been imbued with Christianity, but even so it is clear that he feels more offended by the word *abeed* than by 'Christian dog'.

John turns up in church regularly, sometimes in ours,

sometimes in the Protestant church. Many Christians here feel persecuted. While it is true that in this war the Christians in the south are often the victims, John would never characterize it as a war between Moslem and Christian. He would rather leave God out of it. Someone once asked him what church he belongs to, Catholic, Protestant, or one of those new sects? I will not soon forget his answer: 'I am John Lakrimoi, and God knows me'.

He works as a day-labourer, loading and unloading lorries in the market-place. It is hard work; it could be easily turned into slave work, but John is a strong man, and he is not for sale. Not only is he a strong man, but he is aware and proud of who he is. When a lorry is to be unloaded in the market-place, it is often John who leads the gang of workers. The work is done at John's pace. When an Arab trader starts shouting at the workers as if they were his slaves, John will slow everybody down and look the trader in the eye, and the trader knows that he had better cool it. John is not owned by anybody; not by the government, not by the SPLA, nor by any merchant. A few days ago he said to me, 'I am no slave, no more'.

But at times this same John is full of pain. Then, when he has earned some money, he will be drunk for a couple of days. And when the cock is drunk, he forgets about the hawk. He will get into a row with the soldiers and the police, calling them everything under the sun: yelling that they let themselves be used by the government to oppress their own people; that their corrupt practices one day will catch up with them; that their mothers must be ashamed of having given birth to them. Police and soldiers don't like to be told such things even if they are true. Sometimes he gets a beating. It hurts, but carrying sacks of salt when you are sweating hurts too. John gets arrested, and sleeps it off on the floor of a cell at the police station. He could not care less; at home he sleeps on the floor anyway. He is prepared to put up with the caning, and he sticks to his point: 'You ought not let them use you to oppress your own people!'

John Lakrimoi used to be a soldier himself, but he was no killer. He could not shoot his own people. I ask him:

would it be different if it meant shooting Arabs? He says: 'They don't look on us as humans, but we must not agree with them by behaving like brutes.'

On the radio, the SPLA spreads the news that food convoys are to be resumed. John listens, then chimes in with one of his comments: 'You Americans are queer sticks, aren't you?' I protest I am not an American, and though calling me an American might not be as bad as calling me a Christian dog, I don't consider it a compliment. I am Dutch, and I point this out to John. He replies, 'Six of one, half a dozen of the other. First you supply the government in Khartoum with bullets and rifles to kill us, and then you give food aid for those of us in the south who have not been killed yet.' John makes it look rather simple, but there is some truth in his reasoning.

He has more questions for the Americans and all that lot like them. For instance, he believes we are honestly against apartheid in South Africa. Listening to the radio news it appears the sanctions by the West against South Africa's apartheid regime have had some results. (Next to the SPLA radio, the BBC news is fairly popular in Sudan; it gives John a view of international affairs.) But John wonders why one never hears anything about apartheid in Sudan? Here black southerners have no rights at all, except to be shot. His culture, his land, his religion are taken away from him; his humanity is in no way respected. 'Why is it that you protest against apartheid in South Africa, and not against apartheid in Sudan?' When John asks this I am less inclined to insist that I am Dutch. After all, the Dutch in South Africa initiated apartheid there. I have no clear answer to John's question. As a 'Christian dog' from the West it is possible that feelings of common guilt may have something to do with it. After all, they are our own cousins who were the oppressors in South Africa. They too, as the Arabs here, have claimed to act in the name of God. But I will not even try to explain to John about my guilt by association. It would not go down well with someone who can say quite confidently: 'I am John, and God knows me'. He knows that there is a lot wrong with himself, but he is too free to be determined by feelings of guilt. John's goodness to his fellow man does not come from having to make amends for some wrong, but simply from the fact that he is his fellow man. The apartheid here is not so black-and-white as it is in South Africa. The blacks are often blacker, the Arab oppressors are a shade or two browner than the sun-tanned whites of South Africa. I agree with John; apartheid is a more appropriate name for the problem in Sudan than 'religious war'.

John must be off. After the SPLA news, his siesta is over and he should head for the market-place to see whether there is still a job to be done. He is a proud fellow, by no means a slave. He has got the air of a free man. He fights for that freedom without a gun, but that does not make him less a freedom fighter. This war is not hopeless. I know a man who has set himself free, and John Lakrimoi is his name.

GOD'S HOME

Man cannot command God
Maasai proverb

It is still early in the morning when my friend and I drive through the outskirts of Juba. The huts stand close together as if huddled against the wind and dust. Women walk to the Nile with water-jugs on their heads. The people here are very black, so black that they appear nearly blue, but the children soon take on a drab-grey from the dust kicked up by our car. Still, they keep up their friendly waving at us. The road is like a washboard. In town there are about six miles of tarmac, the only asphalt road in southern Sudan. A few years ago Juba was a minor provincial town of perhaps 60,000 inhabitants. Now, swollen with all the refugee camps, 300,000 people try to survive here.

As we jolt along on the road to the Nile, a majestic building comes into view on our right, atop a small hill. It is quite at odds with its surroundings. A large wall is being built around it, possibly to keep the refugees out. The building would be quite at home in Italy, and in fact it was the Italians who went to great pains to erect this edifice here, on the bank of the river. Large letters on its tower proclaim: *Haec est domus Dei*. My friend tries in vain to avoid the bumps in the road, while I wonder for whom this Latin text has been carved on this building. 'Here is the house of God', or 'This is God's home', is what it means. The Bari, Juba's original inhabitants, do not speak Latin. Nowadays many languages are spoken in the city:

the various tribal languages of the refugees, and the development and aid organizations often use their own
languages. It is not unusual to hear Dutch or Norwegian.
But not Latin. That text cannot be meant for them. The
Italians who built this cathedral did know Latin, that's
true, but being themselves the builders of 'God's Home',
they did not need this indication either. I come to the
conclusion that they must have inscribed the message for
God himself, to give him a clue where his home is. After
all, the building was erected before the Second Vatican
Council, when Roman Catholics addressed and adored
God mainly in Latin. He is bound to understand that
language; at least he must have understood it in those
days. God has had to wander around a long time in Africa,
He has lived in trees and mountains for ages. Missionaries
were not always pleased with a wandering God, so hard
to get hold of, so difficult to control. Here, now, a worthy
house has been put up for him, and he can read on the
tower that this is where his home is, just in case he gets
lost.

We cross the Nile over a clattering Bailey bridge,
donated by the Benelux countries during the short-lived
truce of 1973. There are several refugee camps here. We
call at one of them where my friend is building a water
well. Safe drinking water is very important. Thousands of
people are trying to survive here. Bored to death, men sit
in little groups in the shadow of the sparse trees. On the
other hand, the women have no time to get bored; they
are cooking on small fires or washing clothes; the well
will help them most. Children are playing, messing
around with water, quarrelling or watching with great
interest the two white visitors.

Masudio, a lady teacher who speaks English, shows me
around the camp. Some families have a tent, donated by
one or other non-governmental organization. These tents
are far too hot to live in; they probably were designed for
Scandinavian countries and not for Sudan where the sun
bakes everything below it. Other people have tried to
build their own huts, but at present it is very hard to get
grass. They have started a school for the children under
one of the trees. Masudio tells about the health

programme, which is largely run by the displaced people themselves. The water well under construction is part of this programme. These are positive developments, but the teacher also tells me about the minefields around the camp. The government has put them there to prevent the SPLA soldiers from coming into town. Only recently some women were killed when they were looking for firewood. Because of these minefields the men cannot go hunting nor can they keep cattle, apart from a few goats which are tied to the trees. The displaced people have become prisoners in these camps, and regularly they are accused of supporting the SPLA. The tangible misery makes me quiet.

Masudio tells me about herself. She and her children walked more than sixty-five miles fleeing from the war. She has no idea where her husband is. If he is fighting in the SPLA army, she had just as well say she does not know. The war has been going on for years, and may last for many more. My friend joins us and explains to Masudio how they can prevent the well from getting polluted. She listens carefully and promises that she will explain it to the people. A woman approaches with a request: will she ask us whether she and her sick child can go with us in the car to the hospital in Juba? Without consulting us, Masudio tells the woman that we will indeed take her and her child to Juba hospital. Ordinarily I would resent that permission is presumed, but Masudio is so clearly in charge of everything here that I accept her decision. Officially, one of those men under the tree over there will be the boss, but the teacher is the one who organizes much of what happens here. Through her initiatives she has become the leader. When it comes to work and development it is often the women who take the lead. On the cover of the copybook which lists the names of the schoolchildren, she has written, *The hand that rocks the cradle, should also rock the boat.*

Looking around the camp is depressing. For a long time these people will be dependent on relief. Hardly any cultivation is possible because of the minefields. However, this woman Masudio does not appear depressed at all. I muster up the courage to ask: 'Masudio, how have you coped with this life, for so many years now? I think I just could not do it. It would be my death.' But Masudio is a strong woman in a starved body. She need not think long about an answer: 'We do not bear this alone. God is here with us.' She says this, so utterly convinced, that I cannot but believe her, although in this environment my belief is stretched to the limit. When Masudio and so many others say here, 'God is with us', it conveys great trust. When I begin to feel desperate, they are still full of trust. Trust is probably the very essence of faith. She radiates this trust. I am glad she is here.

The people in the camp do their praying together under one of the trees. Occasionally, a priest comes to celebrate the Eucharist. On Sundays they often go to the cathedral in town, and that is special, different, but as such not a better church than the tree. I have heard the story of the girl who had grown up in the rural area and who, with her community, used to pray under such a tree. She went with her mother to town and her mother took her to a big building and explained to her daughter that this was a church. The child looked around and said, 'But where is the tree?'

We drive back to Juba. My friend the well-builder is not much of a talker. The mother protects her sick child from the dust, and I am left to my own thoughts. I am still pondering Masudio's answer: 'God is with us'. She seems to have experienced it. And perhaps there is something in it; after all, in Egypt, God's Son had also been a refugee. And again, he spent more time with this sort of people, at the periphery of society, than with the officials and priests in the temple. As we drive into Juba again, we pass by the cathedral and it is very quiet there. I find it hard to believe that God lives there now.

However, last Sunday I attended a service in this cathedral. It was so dynamic and full of enthusiasm that I am inclined to think God was present then. I wonder if God had come with Masudio and the other refugees from the camps around Juba. *Haec est domus Dei*, This is the house of God, I read again. Must I believe this, or is Masudio right in insisting that he is there with them in the camps? I am reminded of Shug, a woman in the novel *The Color Purple* by Alice Walker. She finds God amongst the people. She says: 'Be honest, have you ever found God in church? I haven't, I have only found a bunch of people hoping he would show himself to them. The only God I have ever felt in church I had brought along myself. I think other people do the same. They come to church to share God, not to find him.'[1]

When Masudio comes here on Sunday to sing with her choir, so full of faith and trust, then God will come with her, then he will feel at home here. I would go along with Masudio: 'God's home is where the people are'.

[1]Alice Walker, *The Color Purple*, New York, Harcourt Brace Jovanovich, 1982, p. 165.

EMPTY-HANDED

When the moon is not full, the stars shine more brightly.
Buganda proverb

They were starving and almost naked when, in small groups, they reached Tombura. They had been on the move for more than two months, living on what they found in the forest: roots, berries and vegetables growing in the wild. People of another tribe would have succumbed, but the Azande know the forest and the forest is their friend. It protected them against renewed attacks by the SPLA, the freedom fighters in southern Sudan. Most of the displaced are women and children. You can see the fear in their eyes when they tell how the rebels set fire to the grass in which they were hiding. That is how people here hunt wild animals. They set fire to the grass and the fleeing animals are shot. Many of the men were shot. The young ones were captured to be trained as freedom fighters. Nakubeya had jumped to her feet and had shouted to the soldiers, 'You've got our men, you have our sons, let us be so that our tribe won't be wiped out!' To her great surprise she was not killed, the shooting stopped and they had fled into the forest, she and all the women and children. Tired, sick and very down-hearted they have more or less settled in and around the school, which is empty now, for the Christmas holidays.

Tombura has a committee which administers emergency relief for displaced people, but for quite some time there has been nothing to hand out, and so the committee has little to do. We pick up a radio message in Yambio, a cry for help: What is the church going to do for these people? For months we were able to supply seeds and tools to help the refugees and the displaced. After all, the soil around this area is very fertile and rather than build camps for them, we encouraged the displaced families to start their own gardens. Initially, we had some food and blankets too. But now everything has been distributed among other groups of displaced people. New supplies would have to come from Juba, but that is impossible. The roads are minefields, and even if a small plane were to become available, it is getting increasingly risky to fly. We are empty-handed. All we have is a little money, but you cannot eat that, and there is hardly any food left to be bought in Yambio or Tombura.

I go to Médecins Sans Frontières, the French medical organization. In the past they were able to help a few times, but they have practically become refugees themselves. Their little plane, which supplies their hospitals, has been shot down by government troops, and these are doctors who staff government hospitals! If that same government shoots down their plane, can it really care about the health of the people in the south of Sudan? The four people in the plane, three French and a Sudanese, were killed. The people at the MSF compound are shocked. Their organization in France has decided they must leave Sudan. For some it is a relief, but for others, who have been here longer, it only makes things worse. The French doctor at Tombura visited the refugees, but apart from handing out some medicines there wasn't much she could do. Yes, she could listen to their stories. Then she heard on the wireless that her colleagues were leaving Yei because the situation there had become unbearable, because of constant attacks from the SPLA. They call themselves Médicins Sans Frontières (Doctors without borders, without limits), but of course there are always limits. They too feel defeated, empty-handed.

I decide to go to Tombura anyway, with only the meagre gift of money. But now that the aid organizations have nothing to hand out, now that no NGO claims the displaced, a new development has taken place. The local people of Tombura have begun to talk to the refugees.

When strangers meet, they often try to find out whether
they are somehow or other relatives. Everybody in
Tombura, the locals and the refugees, seems to be a relative of everybody else. Perhaps not brother or sister,
father or mother, cousin, brother- or sister-in-law, but at
least they are relatives of those who were brother or
sister, father or mother, cousin, brother- or sister-in-law.
It is said, 'The friends of our friends are our friends.' And
that has made all the difference. Food has been brought
for relatives who come in need. They need no longer be
classified as 'refugees' now that there was no refugee aid.
Being labelled a refugee is often just as disastrous as
being labelled 'on the dole' or 'welfare mother' or
'asylum seeker'. The label 'displaced' is meaningless now,
and so these 'refugees' have become people again.

At the market there was a fresh supply of second-hand
clothes, smuggled from Zaïre for Christmas. The people
bought these clothes for their destitute second cousins or
for the child of their maternal uncle's sister-in-law. A girl
who did not want to go without a Christmas present altogether, donned the new dress herself and gave her old
dress to a girl who was family somehow or other in some
vague way. It was clear to me that injecting money into
this self-help economy would not be right.

Together with Sister Natalia and the French doctor,
Véronique, I visited the new arrivals. We listened to how
they had fled from the SPLA, and Véronique told how the
MSF plane had been shot down and that she might have
to leave the country. Silently, each with our own
thoughts, we walked back to the mission where people
were sweeping the church compound in preparation for
Christmas. All three of us felt at a loss and could find no
more words to encourage each other. I was grateful that
we knew each other well enough to be able to remain
silent.

And then it is Christmas night. Lights are hanging in the
trees around the church, which is too small to accommo-
date the more than 2,000 people who have gathered here.
The altar table has been put outside. People flock around,
the refugees are the guests of honour. The collection
during Mass will be for them, so it has been announced.

Also the doctor and nurses of Médicins Sans Frontières have been specially invited by the people. Chairs are brought for them. On hearing that their colleagues were killed in the plane, the people had expressed their sympathy by bringing a bunch of bananas, or by just sitting on their doorstep and repeating the word '*malesh*', which means much more than 'we're sorry'. It can also mean, 'hard luck, this blow hits you', but it always implies sympathy. It is a small word, instead of many words that would have no heart.

All around the congregation there are police and soldiers, carrying their guns as usual. They stay at the edges of the congregation; their guns are an embarrassment to them, but they have strict orders to remain armed. Tonight they are part of the congregation.

It is a service full of prayers for peace. In his homily, my missionary colleague encourages those who offer a home to the people who have none. Very clearly, this has been happening here these last few days. There is singing, imported Christmas melodies, which connects me with home in Holland. But the local songs are sung with a lot more soul. The collection baskets are passed through the crowd. For the most part the local people have brought food which they send forward to be put in the big hampers: maize, cassava, bananas, a few chickens, and one of the shopkeepers has brought a goat. I put the money, which I brought for the refugees, in one of the baskets; after all, the collection is for them. It is money from an aid organization and it must be accounted for. I wonder what they would say if I were to write in my report to the donor organization: '£500 put in the Christmas collection at Tombura'. Still, I think it is the right thing to do.

During Holy Communion a new rhythm starts on the drums and the African xylophone. Then comes the melody; it is obviously a song that is deeply rooted in this culture. The rhythm slowly takes hold of the congregation. People sing and clap their hands. Some begin to sway with the rhythm, and gradually the two thousand people begin to dance, very slowly at first, as if they are waking out of sleep. The drummers drum faster. The displaced people are especially invited to join in the dance. Doctor Véronique is taken by the hand, she carries a child on her arm. The child is often with her; she has more or less adopted the doctor as her mother, since her own is dead. Véronique dances along, hesitantly at first, but then wholeheartedly, tears rolling down her cheeks. It is as if she is brought back to humanity, returning from the solitude of her sorrow of the past few days. We were empty-handed and did not know what to do, but these people, also empty-handed, have still so much to offer to each other and to us.

I am presiding at this liturgy with another missionary, although it is evidently led not by us but by the people themselves. As the dance continues, my colleague at the altar asks me whether we should call a halt for a final prayer and the blessing. Why should we? This dance is a blessing and a prayer. We give these people our blessing, we bless the dance and join in.

THE PIOUS GUERRILLA
FIGHTER

*Man is like palm-wine, when young, sweet, but
without strength; in old age, strong but harsh.*

Congolese proverb

The first time I met him, it was in the middle of the night.
He was standing in the road, flagging us down. He looked
fierce with his beard, his army fatigues, revolver at the
ready. I stopped and he approached the car looking tough
and impressive, one could smell the guerrilla fighter.
When he saw who we were, he relaxed and his greeting
was very friendly. He had been informed over the radio
that we were on our way to visit Yambio and he told us
that we were welcome.

Yambio is the provincial headquarters of Western
Equatoria. It is named after Chief Yambio, one of the
chiefs of the ancient Azande people. Here in Yambio I
started my work in South Sudan in 1988, when it was still
in the hands of the government. I had left the area at the
end of 1990 before it was liberated by the SPLA. This was
my first visit after the liberation, in which this bearded
fighter, Commander Kuol, had played a leading role.

He called over a few soldiers who brought us glasses of
water. They had prepared accommodation for us, and
there was still hot water for us to take a bath if we wanted.
For a moment I protested, and said that we could go on
to the mission station or the house of the bishop. But
Commander Kuol made it clear to us that we were his
guests that night; we visit the church and the bishop's
house the following day. It was said in a friendly manner,
but at the same time it was clear that we had no option; it

was more or less an order. He showed us to our beds in one of the houses on the main street of Yambio. A few soldiers were sleeping on the veranda in front of the house. I hoped that they had not been ordered to give up their beds for us.

I woke in the morning when Kuol took his jalabia[1] from under the bed in which I was sleeping. It was then I realized that the commander had given up his own bed for us. He was an SPLA soldier, and a Moslem. Washed and dressed in his jalabia, he looked more benign than last night, and he went along to the mosque to say his prayers. Kuol also has a Moslem name, but he finds his tribal name more important.

Yambio has a small mosque, and before the town was liberated by the SPLA at the end of 1991, the Moslem Arab traders had their own imam. Very few of the local population are Moslem, but in the past I never noticed any tension here between Christians and Moslems; they even attended each others' festivals. Few soldiers of the SPLA are of Kuol's faith, but he comes from the Blue Nile province which is predominantly Moslem, so he is Moslem and proud of it.

All that was a few years ago. Recently, Kuol and I recounted our first meeting, and Kuol explained that the Koran asks Moslems to be especially hospitable to guests, or 'sons of the road',[2] as he calls them. They should extend hospitality to non-Moslems too. But that had not been the only reason why he had insisted that we be his guests. He had needed time to clean up the bishop's house, as we were the first to visit the church after the liberation of Yambio. All buildings which had been empty when the SPLA arrived had been requisitioned by the liberators, including the property of the church. The church vehicles were now used by the SPLA. Kuol explained that these cars had been given for Sudan, to serve the people of southern Sudan. All the priests who had used these cars in the past had fled to the Central

---

[1]A jalabia is the white dress which Moslems often wear when they go to the mosque.
[2]Koran 2:177.

African Republic or to Zaïre. Was the SPLA not now serving the people here? Even if this was the case it took a bit of time before I got used to the fact of seeing soldiers drive around in the Land Rover which I used last year. Being still somewhat afraid of this soldier in those days, I had kept silent. But Kuol wanted to talk.

One of the things that he had wanted to know was, why had the priests left when they heard that the SPLA was approaching Yambio? I ventured that there were horrible stories about the SPLA, spread especially by the government troops, stories about looting and killings. Kuol is not touchy in these matters, and rather than defend the SPLA, he fires back at me: are Catholics afraid to die? Moreover, he points out that many of the soldiers who behaved so badly call themselves Christian. He is disappointed with us; he got most of his education in a Christian school and he certainly believes in a life after this one. He expected that we, priests, who talk about heaven, would be less afraid to die. I admit that I preferred to go on living for a while longer. He thinks that we should provide priests for the SPLA, as he considers that it is not right that he, a Moslem, must lead the soldiers in prayer before a battle. Most of his soldiers belong to one or other Christian denomination. I explain that I am not too happy with the way he mixes war and religion. I do not believe in Holy War, Jihad, which is preached by his Moslem brothers in Khartoum.

The Commander does not appreciate my remark. He asks me to remember the Crusades, in which my forefathers had killed his forefathers. Could I defend that? Were those attacks on Islam truly Christian? I allow that I am not particularly proud of that part of our history. He adds that the word Islam comes from the same root as the Arabic word *salaam*, peace. 'Islam' really means 'making peace', he assures me. That is what he is fighting for, peace in his country. He seeks the fourfold peace: peace with God, peace with oneself, peace with one's neighbour, peace with the whole of creation.

I ask Kuol whether he is trying to convert me. He rejoins that he would be satisfied if I did not see in every Moslem a fundamentalist. I promise not to generalize, on

condition that he stops talking about the Crusades. Kuol
goes on to explain that he, as a Moslem, is not proud of
the way in which the government in Khartoum keeps
calling their followers to holy war against the people in
the south. He has studied the Koran and wants me to
know that the jihad of the Koran differs greatly from the
aggressive war this government is waging against the
southern Sudanese. Jihad is a war against pagans to be
taken up if they make it impossible for Moslems to live in
peace, and Kuol and I agree that the people in the south
are not pagans, and that the perpetrators of the war are
often the northern fundamentalists. The fundamentalists
in Khartoum do not let the people of the south live in
peace. Moreover, only a truly holy leader can call for a
jihad, and Kuol thinks the present leaders in Khartoum
are not devoted Moslems. They are power-hungry people
who use Islam to get more power. He points out that
whether the people in the south are Moslem or not, has
very little to do with this war.

This conversation with Kuol was the first of many that
we had over the years. At first, the local people, just like
myself, had been a little afraid of Kuol, because of his
fierce demeanour. He was amused when I told him that
we had been afraid of him. But gradually the people had
come to respect him. Some even started to like him,
because he was a just man who could be relied upon. He
is a soldier not only interested in war, but one who also
tries to understand the social problems behind the war.
He wants to read more about economics because without
it peace will not last. He is a man keen to learn from those
whom he meets.

One of the local women who had joined the movement
fell in love with him, or perhaps it was the other way
round; I am not quite sure how it started. I only remember that during one of my visits to Yambio, Kuol met me
one evening and asked me to buy him a Kaunda suit when
I next went to Nairobi. People often made such requests
of me; what was unusual in the commander's case was
that he came with the money for the dress suit. He
announced that he was going to marry Miriam, whom I
had known as Mary. The whole town was excited about

this marriage between one of the SPLA commanders and a local girl.

That evening Kuol and I had a long talk about marriage. He told me that for a long time he had believed that the missionary sisters were the wives of the missionary priests. Nowadays he believed that this was not the case, and he seemed to pity me, being celibate. Yes, he had heard about religious life. He saw the importance of obedience. He also obeyed orders and he expected his soldiers to obey him. With the vow of obedience he had no quarrel. But an Italian sister had tried to explain to him the vow of poverty, stressing that it meant owning no personal property; that everything belonged to the religious community. Kuol was not impressed; he thought that the missionaries were rich and as far as he was concerned they could be a bit more generous. With regard to the explanation of the sister, Kuol had come to the conclusion that most Africans lived the vow of poverty. Did not being rich mean having a lot to share? But in the eyes of Kuol we had it all mixed up in the Catholic Church. You see, what we call celibacy is, according to Kuol, absolute poverty. A man who does not have wife or children is poor. As a Moslem, Kuol can marry more than one wife, and in his eyes I am poverty-stricken, even if I have all the material goods in the world. Smiling, he adds that he is also a bit of a missionary, and that he has an advantage over me, for often Moslems spread their religion through trade and marriage.

As the weeks and months passed, the town of Yambio became more accessible, and non-governmental organizations became interested in starting all kinds of relief programmes, especially when people started trickling back from Zaïre. But relief organizations have their own rules which often do not exactly dovetail into the local way of life, in this case, that of the Azande people. People had to be registered as living in refugee camps, since that was simpler for the relief distribution system. This prevented people from finding land, necessarily at a distance from the camps, and starting their own gardens. Kuol was furious. The SRRA had accommodated the NGOs, and now another delegation was coming to take photographs which they needed for their fundraising. For this they needed a permit from the SPLA. One of the officers made the request to Kuol when I happened to be in his office. The commander was unco-operative, and I had to smile when he said: 'The world seems to think that Africa is just a zoo. We don't need any more people who just want to come and look. Putting these people in camps is like putting animals in cages.'

That evening Kuol visits me; he is obviously still unhappy with the approach of the relief organizations, who all follow a distribution system which has been thought out in a far-away country, without taking the local people into account. The givers decide who is in need, and very often they decide that the ones in need are those who can be reached easily. Kuol tells me that this is very wrong according to the Koran, where the poor and the needy have a special place. He knows his Koran better than I my Bible. We talk at length and conclude that both Christians and Moslems do not always live up to their holy books.

He has another problem. He has organized the soldiers to cultivate their own gardens in an attempt at self-sufficiency, but it will take time before the harvest is ready. His soldiers have to eat, and the SPLA is taxing the people to provide food. It causes tension between the SPLA and the local people. Kuol must make the decision: either he has to tax the people, which in practice means taking food from them by force, or he has to commandeer food from the relief organizations. He wants my advice, which I refuse, but secretly I hope that he will take part of the relief food. Most countries and organizations send delegations to monitor their relief donations to make sure that no food goes to combatants. But these same countries often provide the weapons and ammunition. A hungry soldier with a gun is more dangerous than a hungry soldier without a gun. It bothers Kuol that it is often easier to get weapons for his soldiers than to get food for them. The relief programmes are often the most difficult programmes to handle, but also the most difficult ones to ignore. How can people help themselves when all they think about is food? Even for a soldier the belly is more important than war. Give them food and they can put their heads to work for more constructive developments. It bothers me that I cannot come out and say: 'Take some of the food which is being supplied by the churches', but in my heart I hope that he will do that rather than take it from the people who hardly have enough to feed themselves.

Now we know each other better, and in some ways have become friends, without having to admit it. Kuol has become rather critical of the churches, and at the same time I seldom praise Islam or the SPLA. In his office he is the tough commander, and I sound pretty unbending when I have to speak as the representative of the Council of Churches. But when we sit together in the evening we regularly admit that we often feel a lot smaller than we pretend. The history of the Church has been sometimes less than glorious, and I can understand Kuol's disappointment in us. But he is also disappointed with the divided SPLA and the government in Khartoum, which claims to act in name of Islam. Maybe Kuol and I can talk together because we can admit that over the years we have all made mistakes.

We wonder together about the fundamentalism in both Islam and Christianity. Kuol thinks that it is rooted in fear and that it grows especially in times of turmoil. We agree that a Catholic fundamentalist is just as dangerous as a Moslem fundamentalist. Religious bigotry of all colours has exerted a great deal of influence in this war. Kuol asks me whether I still think Catholicism is the only right religion. I tell him I have never thought it, although I was taught that this was so when I was young. I add that some Moslems claimed a similar ascendancy in the past. Does he believe that Islam is the only way? Kuol claims no such thing, but with a smile adds, 'Islam is not the only true religion, but it is still the best for me'.

Kuol and I have spoken about the dialogue between Moslems and Christians in Sudan. We are not very optimistic about it. Too much has happened in the past and is still happening now. We have come to the conclusion that any fruitful dialogue is too much to hope for. Or could it be that the meetings between Kuol and myself are precisely part of that dialogue?

BISHOP PARIDE TABAN

The lion says: 'It belongs to me.'
The lioness says: 'Let's share it.'

Haya proverb

It is burning hot when the small plane touches down on the dusty airstrip in Torit. The security official checks our papers under the wing of the plane, the only shade there is. His T-shirt has an exhortation printed on the back: *Brothers and sisters, help each other in these difficult times.* I wonder if it is one of the SPLA slogans. They have this area under control at the moment, and are trying to put it on its feet again. They come up with all kind of slogans to motivate the people to build up their lives again. But below the text are the dates: *24th May 1964–24th May 1989*, and although the struggle for freedom has lasted already more than twenty-five years, the SPLA's fight for a new Sudan started only in 1983. Apparently the security officer's T-shirt is not of the SPLA.

When the official sees in my papers that Bishop Paride Taban has invited me, he suddenly becomes much friendlier. He explains that Paride Taban is a good friend of his, in fact the bishop gave him this very T-shirt he is wearing. With some pride he shows the front of the T-shirt: the bishop's coat of arms with the text: *God is Love*; below the text there is the picture of an African open fire, as if that love of God must be kept warm. I do not recognize the picture above the text. But Francis (now that we have a common friend the official's name is suddenly made known to me) explains to me that it represents a child's cap from the Madi tribe, to which the bishop belongs.

Such a cap protects the babies from too much sun or from rain and wind. In this picture it looks as if the cap must protect God's love, which might get scorched too in the burning sun, or blown about in rain and wind. Francis wishes me a good time in the liberated area of Sudan. He thinks he does not need to keep an eye on me any further: I will be quite safe in the bishop's hands.

I had met Bishop Paride in Juba a few years ago. At that time he was making frantic efforts to organize a food-convoy to Torit, a town that was being besieged and starved by the SPLA. Many people considered it to be a hazardous enterprise. But this bishop, with his worried look and a beard like an untrimmed hedge, wanted to be with his people. He was the Bishop of Torit, and that is where he wanted to be, although he was well aware of the danger there. He was prepared to face that danger for the people of Torit, who were threatened with starvation.

They set off with over seventy lorries under the much-needed protection of the army. It is not a long distance: eighty-four miles from Juba to Torit. The road, however, was a minefield. They often had to find themselves a new track. The SPLA considered it to be a military convoy and attacked it constantly. It took thirty-one horrible days and nights to cover that distance. Many were killed, soldiers and civilians. Paride buried them with just a simple prayer. Lorries hit mines or were shot to smithereens by the SPLA, who were using the hunger of the people in Torit to conquer that town. For nearly all his life as a priest it has been war for Bishop Paride. But he will not accept hunger as a weapon.

As last he reached Torit, with many wounded, and twenty lorries fewer than they had started with. The town was starving. People were eating dogs and cats; a single rat cost $6. The food supplies brought hope, at least for a while. The bishop brought them new courage: he shared the people's sorrow, he shared in their hunger. But the supplies ran out. When the people were too weak even to dig graves for those around them who had died of starvation, the bishop gave his last gallons of diesel fuel for the road-builders' bulldozer. It was used to dig a mass grave, where day by day new bodies were buried.

Torit was cut off from the outside world, only the bishop had his radio transmitter. One of his messages before Torit was conquered said: 'We are asking the people to make their preparations for a good death. All that we can offer them in Torit is our sweat, blood and our tears.' Perhaps Churchill who said something like that inspired this statement, but this bishop saw a lot more sweat, blood and tears than Churchill.

Even the government army had no more food, and it was fortunate that the SPLA managed to conquer Torit when it did. The famished army could no longer stop them. The SPLA took Bishop Paride Taban prisoner; after all, he had fed the army too, and he had been critical of the war methods of the SPLA. True, he would not let a man die of starvation just because that man was a soldier. You will not hear him say he was ill-treated by the SPLA. During imprisonment he made many friends, not only among his fellow-prisoners, but also among his SPLA jailers. With all of them he celebrated, very soberly, the silver anniversary of his ordination to the priesthood. He was released after one hundred days, his weight down to under a hundred pounds, but he was unbroken. After his release he celebrated his silver jubilee once more, a free man, together with his people. On that occasion he received those T-shirts with his coat of arms as a present, and he gave them to his friends instead of a commemoration card.

Tonight I am the guest of Bishop Paride Taban. With some of his African priests we sit on small folding chairs under the guava trees in front of his house. He sits here nearly every evening with his visitors. It is cooler out than inside, but he also sits here because the people will more readily come along to say hello when they hear him laugh. Everyone is welcome. If there is tea, you can have a cup of tea; otherwise you get just a glass of water. He tells us about his recent journey to Europe, where he went to plead for more solidarity with southern Sudan. He returned a few days ago. His beard is neatly trimmed and with a big smile he pats his belly when he discloses that his weight has returned to his normal 130 pounds. You can tell from his face that he is happy to be back home again. He drove himself through the three days it takes from Nairobi to Torit. A young priest who came with him says the bishop nearly fell asleep, but Paride waves that away with a smile.

For him, driving a car is relaxation. He would rather drive an old Land Rover than govern a diocese. He has the oldest car in the diocese, which only he manages to keep on the road. He was a mechanic and driver before he started his studies for the priesthood. As a driver he learned how to improvise. When the road is bad or a bridge has disappeared, you need great prudence and patience in finding a new way through the bush or the river. He has got something of the rascal about him when talking about his driving adventures. He never had any ambition to become a bishop. When he was asked to become a bishop, he replied: 'What will become of the church if they appoint a truck-driver rather than a theologian as bishop?' But his diocese too has had a very difficult way to go, and it has not been badly off with Paride at the wheel, steering his diocese through harsh and difficult times.

Yesterday we talked together about the reconstruction of southern Sudan after this long war. Much has been destroyed, but that is not the first worry. Paride wants to co-operate with other churches in providing for the people. People must be given a new incentive; they themselves are in need of reconstruction. That is why he started, together with Bishop Nathaniel Garang of the Anglican Church, a council of churches for the liberated area. We had been looking over some destroyed buildings yesterday, when we came to the market-place where people were dancing. They danced around us and the bishop danced a few steps with them. As we continued our way he said: 'Oh well, buildings *are* needed, but they can't dance. People can dance.'

Tonight he tells about his visit to Norway. Many Norwegians worked here before the war. They had their own village where the families engaged in development work lived. Their housing was comfortable, they had electricity and running water, even their own swimming pool. This village was destroyed in the battle around Torit. The

Norwegians who lived there know Paride and gave him a
great welcome when he arrived in Norway. 'What is left of
what we built up in the Sudan?' they asked. The bishop
smiles a bit when he tells his answer: 'Of what you built
up? Yes, some have died of starvation or were killed in the
war, but most of them are still alive, and send you their
kindest regards.' The Norwegians did not dare to ask
further about their buildings. The following day they
wanted to talk business; they wanted to discuss projects,
money, and contracts. Bishop Paride, however, is not only
a businessman. Money and material help alone do not
mean solidarity to him. Instead of a straight answer with
figures and statistics, the bishop gave them the story
which he begins telling us now, about an almost desperate mother during the war around Torit. And there is no
longer that rakish, cavalier air about him. His eyes betray
his concern.

The mother has no food left for her children. The pots
in her hut are empty, but only she knows it. The children
just trust Mama. They are poor but don't know it. She
tells the children she has to cook, but that it will be trou-
blesome if they are around when she unpacks the dried
meat from the pot at the back, so the kids are sent
outside. The meat pot is empty. She fills the cooking pot
with stones and water and puts it on the fire. Then she
calls the children back in and asks them to keep the fire
going. Dried meat takes a long time to cook, and the children, thinking they are cooking meat, forget all about
being hungry. The mother goes into the woods to find
food, but, as many others have discovered, there is little
remaining there. The basket on her head remains empty,
and she is desperate. Suddenly, from nearby she hears a
lion roar. She is scared to death of lions, yet she draws
closer to the sound and from behind a tree she watches a
lion devouring a buffalo. Oh, she is afraid, but she also
knows that the meat will keep her children alive. She
takes the circlet of grass, with which she balances her
basket, from her head and flings it at the lion to divert its
attention. It works. When the lion pounces on the grass
ring, the mother throws sand on the buffalo meat,
knowing that lions do not eat soiled flesh. When the lion

returns, it recoils from its meal. The mother fills her basket with the soiled flesh, goes to wash it in the river and runs home. The children are still minding the fire. She sends them out again and quickly cooks the fresh meat, which does not take long. Her children and those of the neighbours have something to eat that day. Only the mother knows how close they had been to starvation.

When Bishop Paride told this to the Norwegians they had hung on every word, as we did now. But the bishop had not stopped there, and had elucidated: 'This is not just the story about a mother in Torit. It is also the story of our present-day world. The West is that lion. You have control of the buffaloes that can save the lives of many.'

I do not know if many bishops feel themselves to be mothers. It is certain that not many African men compare themselves with women, but the bishop had added: 'Yes, and I, as I am here now, feel somewhat like that mother'.

AS STRONG AS WHAT?

*Cross the river in a crowd and the
crocodile won't eat you.*

Madagascar proverb

The church in Yambio is packed with people; everybody
has come today. But then, today is a special occasion. It is
nearly six months since Holy Mass was last celebrated
here. Then, as the SPLA approached, many people who
had government jobs and also the priests fled from the
force of arms to the Central African Republic or Zaïre. The
expatriates, including myself, had been the first to leave.
Only the common folk, who possessed nothing and there-
fore had nothing to lose, stayed behind. Many of them
had hid in the forest. No one knew what this liberation by
the SPLA entailed. Here in Yambio it was not so bad;
nobody was killed. In other places it was quite different.

The people gave us a warm welcome when we arrived
here a few days ago and we spent two long days listening
to them. They told us about the ransacking by the retreat-
ing government troops. Some of the Arab traders had
booby-trapped their shops before joining the fleeing
government troops. Then there was the frightening
waiting for the liberators, the SPLA, about whom such
terrifying stories had been told. The looting of the Arab-
owned shops by the SPLA and the civilians had ended in a
fight over the spoils. The people got into a fuddle of
excitement and looted everything, including the mission
and the bishop's house. Then came the sobering up:
'What have we done?'

They told us of their disappointment that the priests

had fled. No, they did not offer this as justification for looting the mission, but without the priests and their bishop and the civil servants, the town was given over to mob rule. Nobody knew in which direction to go. Families were disrupted. Half a family fled to Zaïre and the other half was too late to get away and had stayed in Yambio. They showed us the bishop's ransacked house. In the room that had once been mine, there was a cupboard forced open, papers strewn all over. They had not taken my breviary, but it was left to be eaten by ants.

It is a few days since Bishop Paride Taban, Matthew Samusa, a Sudanese priest, and I arrived here. Over the radio several pleas for help had been sent to us in Torit. Last year this area was my field of work, and so Bishop Paride thought I was the man to go and find out in what way the churches could help in the district. I am not much of a hero; I did not know whether it would be possible to get here. In Maridi heavy fighting was still going on, and I would have to go through that town in order to reach Yambio. The bishop saw my doubts and, after consulting his vicar-general, offered to come with me. With him, I would dare to try. It happens often that he gives me the courage to venture on roads I would not try alone.

Over a week ago we set out from Torit in a Toyota Landcruiser. Some people told us the journey was impossible. Bishop Paride answered: 'We can only say it is impossible when we have tried. No one has tried so far.'

The first days through North Uganda were not without problems, but we made progress every day. It was only at Rosiulu, a small town between Yei and Maridi, that the real problems began. When we approached this small town, SPLA soldiers shouted at us to get off the road as quickly as possible. As I steered to the side of the road, our car was completely covered with branches by the soldiers. When we got out of the car we saw a bomber circling overhead and we ran for cover into the bush. When we heard the plane departing we left our cover and the soldiers congratulated us for arriving safely in Rosiulu. Now we had a chance to look around. There was a big army camp of grass huts along the road. The soldiers, poorly dressed but well armed, explained that the battle for Maridi was in full swing. The government had been trying to bomb them the last few days. At the same time the government was trying to supply its troops in Maridi from the air. Planes dropped food and ammunition in Maridi for the government troops and with their bombs they tried to bombard SPLA positions.

A young commander receives us. Yes, he does know Bishop Paride Taban. Everybody in South Sudan seems to know him. Yes, he had heard on the radio that we were on our way and he thinks our intention to visit the church in Yambio is very praiseworthy. Still this man looks worried, as if he would have been much happier if we had not come. He is responsible for our safety. He asks us to give him some time, and meanwhile to be his guests. We are given a captain's quarters: a grass roof, a bed made from a few sticks in the ground, with a contraption that looks like a mattress made from papyrus reeds. The food is very simple, although they probably offer us the best they have.

Every now and then the commander visits us; the government troops are trying to escape from Maridi and he does not want us to run into them. For a moment we consider returning to Uganda and trying to reach Yambio through Zaïre. I see from the commander's face that it is a bad idea; he starts talking in Arabic to the bishop. Later I hear that on no account would he have let us go back along the road as I might betray their position. But he also tells us that he has been in touch with Dr John Garang himself, the chairman of the liberation movement, who has promised to find a way through for us.

For two days we live next to the ammunition bunkers while the bombers circle over our heads. It makes me restive and a bit nervous, but Paride is quite calmly practising a kind of 'palaver' apostolate among the soldiers. They talk about their families at home, they talk about this war; the soldiers are excited about capturing Maridi one of these days, but the bishop doubts whether there is a military solution to this war. He fully understands they want to win the war, but are they not forgetting to win the people as well?

Then, as evening falls, the commander comes to inform us that we can continue our journey to Yambio. A lorry with soldiers will drive ahead of us. The soldiers explain that I must keep exactly to the lorry's tracks, even when the road gets bad. A few days ago a Land Rover ran into a mine. The lorry driver knows this road and thinks he can pick a way through the mines, although one never can be certain. I am at the wheel and feel very uncertain. When Paride Taban notices this, he says: 'If a mistake is going to be made here, it had better be made by a Sudanese'. He offers to do the driving and I let him. Very calmly he follows the lorry in front of us. It is a road with many obstacles: we get stuck in a river, but manage to get out. Several times we leave the main track and we follow a path through the bush. In the distance, near Maridi, we hear an occasional gunshot.

Then, on a sharp tree-stump, the lorry gets a blow-out; it sounds like a shot in the night. From the bushes there is shooting all around us. The soldiers on the lorry have their guns at the ready, but do not return fire. We have put out the lights and use a flashlight to mount the spare tyre. The firing is getting closer; I think of the fleeing government troops, and I am scared. I feel the fear right in my bowels. Now I understand how the expression, 'It scares the living shit out of him', came into the English language.

Bishop Paride Taban stands beside the car, quiet, but very much on the alert. The firing must be from the SPLA, he thinks, otherwise the soldiers who are with us would be much more frightened. The soldiers whisper as they discuss the situation, and when the firing is on top of us they begin to sing loudly one of the SPLA military songs. The bullets cease singing around us and the attackers smile as they appear from the shrubs. Yes, they had not been sure whether these were their own troops or the enemy's. They smile even more when told that they scared the wits out of that white man, me. A bit sheepishly I smile too. Fortunately, at Maridi it has been made clear that it is we who are coming, and not the enemy. Again we switch our lights off and we wait.

Then there is a radio message from Dr Garang himself.

'In a couple of minutes, I'm going to chase these rats into their holes, and then you start driving. The government troops will have no time to fire at you, but whatever happens, keep driving.' The bishop nods; he has driven at the front before. But that he is not quite at ease is clear from the fact that he shakes hands with me and says: 'Garang's guns cannot protect us in the end; let's put our trust in the Lord'.

Suddenly a tremendous bombardment bursts out over Maridi and I can well imagine that every government soldier runs for safety into the shelters, having no time to fire at us. I would have liked to run into a dugout myself, but we are already on our way. The bishop follows the slithery track of the lorry. He cannot resist a smile when he sees me duck when another shell explodes over Maridi. I really wonder where he finds his strength and courage. It takes us more than half an hour to get through and around Maridi, protected by the shelling that goes on over our heads.

And so, relieved, we find ourselves on the road to Yambio. 'This is your home', says Paride, 'You know the way here better than me', and leaves me to do the driving; he refreshes himself with a few sips of water, and we continue our trip through the night to Yambio. I tell him that never in all my years in Africa have I been so scared as in the past few hours. He says something about not being able to do anything about fear: one must respect it. I ask him if he is never afraid. He does not give a direct answer. He just looks ahead. Maybe he thinks I should not ask things like that, but he lays his hand on my shoulder and allows me to share some of what goes on in his mind. Like every African he loves life. 'Life is a very precious gift. If you grasp it or hold on to it with all your might, you will crush it. Hold it loosely in your hands, grateful for the gift, not in a forced manner. Oh, it's true that it may slip away from you, but then at least you have not been the one to crush it.'

I ask him if he is reminding me of the Bible which also says something about he who tries to save his life, will lose it. It makes him laugh, but he thinks it interesting that Christ confirms what he has discovered, and what so many Africans know. Life is not just in our own hands. Then he sits back in his seat and five minutes later I notice that he has gently fallen asleep.

All that happened a few days ago. Now we stand face to face with the well-filled church in Yambio. The soldiers have come too. Paride starts his sermon. Almost timidly he thanks everyone for the warm welcome. He explains that we have not come with a carload of promises. 'We have come to share God with you.' A high-ranking soldier looks disappointed. Maybe he had expected something else. Earlier, the SPLA had requested medicine, seeds, school materials and lots of emergency relief. Paride speaks of making room in your heart for love. He tells them that he is well aware of all that happened here, and he does not gloss over it. He talks of making up with each other and forgiving each other. He can do this, because everyone knows that he has forgiven the SPLA, who held him prisoner. He does not only speak of those that were killed, but of all the kinds of death caused by the war. All the sorrow and grief caused to people, the robberies, the broken relationships, all the suffering that cannot be undone: all these Paride calls 'corpses'. The corpses should not be left lying around; they must be buried. 'We bury our dead with respect and we don't forget them', he adds.

He descends from the sanctuary into the church aisles, stands among the people and explains that now the time has come for them to be strong, to stick together, to stand firm. All timidity has disappeared from his person, he is a stalwart figure in their midst as he explains what he means by being strong: often people do not know what strength they need. They throw a ball on the hard floor or against a wall and it bounces back into their faces. They throw harder and the ball bounces above their heads. Frustrated, they take a stone and throw it: the stone breaks or the floor breaks, or both. Is that the sort of strength we need to build up a new life? Paride thinks it is not and neither do the people who see about them the ruins that resulted from a fight to the finish. No, he does not believe in the 'as strong as iron' or 'as hard as a rock' approach. I am wondering what soft and strong image, at once yielding, soft and strong, he will come up with. The people too are hanging on his lips. 'We must be as strong as what?' he muses, and after a pregnant pause he answers his own question: 'I think we must be as strong as cotton wool!' The people here grow the cotton from which cotton wool is made, not what they would consider the most obvious symbol of strength. But Paride repeats: 'We must be as strong as cotton wool! Throw a ball into a heap of cotton fluff and it will not bounce back into your face; throw a stone and the stone will not break, neither will the floor.' And he goes on about the fluff of the cotton plant they all know. Not far from here, in Nzara, there was for many years a thriving cotton industry. When the cotton ball is spun, you can make the strongest rope for binding things together. Didn't they once make canvas in Nzara strong enough to hold off the heaviest rain? Some people nod in recognition. The bishop explains that, just like cotton wool, people too have great potential. Bishop Paride asks a lot from his people, he asks them to be spun and be woven together. He asks them to be as strong as cotton wool.

It is very quiet in the church and within me too, when he brings his sermon to an end with a prayer by Bishop Zubeir of Khartoum, who comes from this area: 'Lord, you became human in our midst; don't let us be turned into stones'.

BARANI ANGELO

Lower your head modestly while passing,
and you will harvest bananas.

Congolese proverb

For a brief moment he hesitated this morning when he
was the guest of honour at our table. The table had been
set by an Italian sister. We missionaries usually eat with
knife and fork. Angelo took the knife and fork in his
hands, paused, and then replaced them and took up a
spoon. The spoon was a compromise for Angelo, who
usually eats with his hands. When he noticed that I saw
his hesitation, he smiled and said, 'Barani Mathew, I am
only a simple catechist, not used to being the guest of
honour of missionaries'. This 'simple' catechist is not so
young any more, close to sixty, I guess. He has been in the
service of the church with the Comboni missionaries for a
long time. His beard resembles the beard of many an
Italian missionary. He is of service to the church without
being servile. He is becoming the wise old man who is
consulted by the local people and the missionaries alike.

A few hours ago Angelo had welcomed the missionaries
back to the parish which they had fled a year earlier.[1] For
many it was a very emotional return. During the celebration of a very solemn and long High Mass, Angelo had said
a word of welcome to the old missionary who in Italy still
had talked about 'my' parish and 'my' people in Sudan.
And for him that was the truth; he loved the people here.

---

[1]The return of the missionaries was celebrated in Nzara on 24
November 1991.

He had spent most of his life in Sudan; when he had to leave the south in 1964, he went to work in the north for some time, but as an old man he had returned to Nzara. That is where he was when he and others had to flee last year. There had been a moment of comedy this morning when the missionary and Angelo were inviting each other to speak first, as if they did not know any longer who was really in charge here. When the priest stepped aside, Angelo had welcomed us and the people who had come from all the outstations to celebrate the return of the missionaries; one old priest and three sisters.

I am present as a visitor. I used to be stationed in this area, but now I also work for the NSCC, the New Sudan Council of Churches. Angelo had welcomed me yesterday at the airstrip. The sisters had brought some food from Nairobi, but the people have welcomed them with more food than they can eat. They have brought chickens, sweet potatoes, groundnuts and plenty of oranges. The people are coming out of the forest where they have been hiding for months. The fact that the missionaries have returned is a sign that it is safe again to live here in Nzara.

After this, Angelo had told us what had happened after the missionaries who, on the advice of the government, fled from the advancing SPLA troops who liberated this area a few days later. Angelo remembers it well. In the night of 25–26 November the SPLA reached Nzara. Not only the missionaries had fled, full of doubt and torn apart, but also the local priest and many people, who had heard horrible stories about the SPLA as liberators; all had fled to Zaïre or the Central African Republic. The old missionary was deeply moved and thanked Angelo for all he had done during the past year.

Angelo had stayed behind. He had helped the missionaries to pack, received the keys of the mission and remained there as its guardian. He does not talk as if he performed an act of courage. Angelo is in many ways a very humble man. For him, it was the obvious thing to do; after all, he was experienced in this field. Angelo knows that the missionaries leave when the situation becomes really dangerous. No, Angelo does not blame them for it, because he has known that things are like that since his youth.

As early as 1964 Angelo saw the missionaries leave when the Sudanese government proclaimed the Missionary Act, which forced the missionaries to leave the south of Sudan. At that time, Angelo was a simple catechist, as he calls himself. Most of his life was spent in the service of the church. The Italian Comboni missionaries gave him the Italian name Angelo when they baptized him in Lirangu leprosy hospital where Angelo's mother was a patient. The missionaries were regular visitors to the hospital and Angelo got to know them and they got to know him. I don't know whether one of these missionaries called Angelo to become a priest or whether he felt called himself. One thing I do know; Angelo went to the seminary in Bussere, near Wau. He was still very young and the seminary was far from home and there was hardly any forest there. Angelo was clever enough as a student, but his health was not too good: his legs were often swollen as they are today. It was at a time when missionaries, themselves often from strong peasant stock, thought that God only called physically strong men to the priesthood. This was a rule not only in Africa; I remember that in my own student days a fellow student had to leave the seminary because he suffered from varicose veins.

The missionaries sent Angelo home to Lirangu. Angelo told me a few years ago about it, saying, 'For more than a year I kept my vocation at home, and I cherished it'. And I have not asked Angelo what he meant by that sentence, but I suppose he did not start a relationship with a girl-friend in the hope that he would be able to return to the seminary. But his health did not improve, and Angelo started to assist the local missionary in teaching his own people as a catechist. He worked well with the missionaries; he was liked for what he himself calls his simplicity. No, Angelo cannot be called a proud man.

It was not an easy time for the people in the south of Sudan. It was the time of the first civil war, the *Anya-nya*, in which the Azande people, to whom Angelo belongs, played an important role. Angelo was more of a church servant than a soldier. When, in 1964, the missionaries left, Angelo helped them to pack and stayed behind as catechist in Lirangu. Not long afterwards, many of the people, with most of the priests, fled to the Central African Republic and Zaïre. Again Angelo stayed behind to serve the people who remained. There is no blame in Angelo's story; he does not judge others easily. He just did what he had to do. He buried the baptismal registers and the mass vestments in such a way that they could not be eaten by the white ants, which have devoured so many of the Sudanese monuments of the past. He would regularly travel to Zaïre to report to the priest on the needs of the people. As they themselves were not prepared to go back to Sudan, they in the end gave Angelo permission to baptize his catechumens. When Angelo told me about this a few years ago, we had laughed about the fact that we had both started our apostolic career at about the same time. When I was struggling in Kenya with my first African language, Angelo was baptizing people in Lirangu. On the commemoration card for my ordination in 1963 I quoted the Letter to the Hebrews: 'Every high priest is chosen from his fellow-men and appointed to serve God on their behalf'. If that applies to me as a priest, then it also applies to Angelo, especially to him who is not judgemental of others. As the author of the Letter to the Hebrews continues: 'Since he himself is weak in many ways, he is able to be gentle with those who are ignorant and make mistakes'.[2] Angelo is a very understanding man. Here is a man fulfilling a ministry proper to its own state, not secondary to, nor opposed to the ordained ministry in the church. I wonder where the church in Sudan would be without the catechists?

But Lirangu was not any longer a safe place to stay; most people, including the leprosy patients, fled to Nzara. 'What was to be done? Should a shepherd not be with his flock?' Angelo had asked himself. And that is how Angelo became catechist in Nzara. Among catechists he was not exceptional in this. In many other parts of southern Sudan the church blossomed under the leadership of the catechists. They usually did not receive a salary, but culti-

---

[2]Hebrews 5.1–2

vated their fields like everybody else. True, now and again the catechumens helped with weeding, and it was not uncommon that Angelo would receive a chicken at the time of a baptism. Angelo and the many other catechists lived closer to the people than the missionaries or even the local priests ever could. He became a leader of his people. But in 1972 the local priests and a few missionaries returned, and Angelo welcomed them and handed the mission back to them again. It often happens in Sudan that one receives formal training following many years' experience. Angelo went for a short time to Juba to take a course in catechetics. He is very grateful that he had that chance to investigate the Bible in depth. Angelo loves to tell Bible stories and in his own way he puts them in the context of every-day life. He returned to Nzara where I met this 'simple' catechist for the first time in 1988.

Regularly Angelo and I would meet in the catechetical centre at the edge of the forest. We would talk together. In one way or another he was very interested in the story of my life and that gave me the right to inquire about his. He would talk about his wife and children. It took some time before he told me that these children of his were all adopted from relatives. He had no children of his own. In this situation, many other men would have taken a second wife. Angelo can understand that and he does not judge such men, but as head catechist he remained faithful to the wife whom he had married long ago. Priests would come to Nzara for a few years and then they would leave, but Angelo remained. The new priest often would have been helpless without him.

After the exodus of the foreign missionaries in 1990, Angelo knew what he had to do. Wood already touched by fire is not hard to set alight. He locked the house of the sisters and the priests and buried some of the fuel and supplies which had been left in the stores of the mission. When the SPLA drew closer, the people took to the forest. Angelo stayed in the mission and every morning he would beat the big wooden drum to let the people know that he was well and still at his post. When the feared liberators, the SPLA arrived, Angelo put on his white cassock and welcomed them. He opened all the doors for them, so that they did not have to break them down, as they had in many other places. 'They only took what they needed', Angelo told me later. I still have the impression that they needed quite a lot as I survey the ransacked mission. But Angelo explains that the local people also looted the mission, and he is inclined to defend the SPLA.

With no priest left in the diocese, Angelo started his apostolate again. He led the people in prayer services. On his old bicycle and with his bad legs he visited not only the outstations but also the neighbouring missions. For the people he became a respected church leader. Among the SPLA he was highly respected and they gave him the title *Abuna*; it means Father, and it is usually the title of a priest. The local people have started to address him as *Barani*, the Azande title for a priest. Angelo never asked to be addressed like that; a simple catechist does not insist on titles.

It is about half a year since I visited Nzara with Bishop Paride Taban. We were the first visitors from outside after the liberation of the area by the SPLA. Again it was Angelo who had received us, and he had asked the bishop for permission to baptize the many catechumens. No Eucharist had been celebrated and Angelo asked us to consecrate enough hosts, so that he could take Holy Communion to the outstations and the neighbouring parishes. Not long after us a Comboni sister, Sr Natalia Gomes, had visited Nzara from Zaïre to see whether the time was ripe to return and work here again. Angelo also made her welcome. Now the missionaries are back and we are celebrating the fact today, and Angelo is the guest of honour. I ask Angelo about the past year; how did he survive, he and the people of Nzara?

But Angelo is an Azande and they hardly ever give you a direct answer. Angelo licks his fingers (he has set aside that spoon). He wipes his beard and starts his story. He is quite solemn, formal, as he talks. I have heard him talking like this when he is teaching his catechumens.

'The Church, the Body of Christ, that is us, went through a very hard time here in Nzara and other places in Western Equatoria. We were crucified. We were cut off from the rest of the world. The people outside must have thought that we were dead. Many people, including the priests, had fled like Christ's disciples on Good Friday. They had been afraid that this was the end. Yes, it was as if we were in the grave, cut off from everybody with no access to the sacraments. Then six months ago Bishop Taban and Barani Mathew arrived, and it was as if they rolled away the stone from the grave. We did not feel as dead as before. We hoped and waited for our priests and missionaries to return. We waited and we prayed, and we prayed and we waited. And then all of a sudden Sister Natalia arrived from Zaïre.' Angelo glances over at Sister Natalia who is with us today, and he goes on, 'Your visit, Natalia, was like Mary Magdalene visiting the open grave. Mary Magdalene talked to the gardener and saw that we, the Church, were alive and she rushed back to Zaïre and to Nairobi to tell everybody the good news, that the Church here is very much alive. Her good news gave you the courage to come back. And we are very grateful that soon our bishop will be back and that our Church will be complete again.'

We all chuckle about this biblical analogy of Angelo, but people often laugh when they don't know what to say. Angelo reads his Bible continually, and from that Bible he tries to understand his own life and the story of his people. It has struck me how closely many people in Sudan identify with the stories in the Bible.

Angelo tells us how he had buried the barrel of fuel which he had returned to the sisters yesterday morning; that amuses the table. But he has a more interesting, far-reaching story: how in every outstation he started communal gardens for the support of the church. In that way, the church and chapels had been able to care for the poor and the leprosy patients, without the aid of the missionaries. He had started to make the church self-supporting. This also happened in other parts of the south of Sudan. Western money is not always a help. So often we missionaries underestimate the resourcefulness of the local people. I remember praising the people in Upper Nile, where for more than ten years no priest had been able to visit the area. I told them that they had done a tremendous job, in spite of the fact that they had no priest or missionary to guide them. After our meeting one of the church leaders had corrected me and said: 'You say that we have done well in spite of the fact that we did not have the support of the priests. I think we have done well thanks to the fact that no priests and missionaries were here. Now we were challenged to take responsibility ourselves and that is what we have done.' That is straightforward Nuer talk. Angelo, an Azande, is a lot more diplomatic than that.

We listen to the many stories of Angelo and we celebrate the return of the missionaries, but we also celebrate this 'simple' catechist. Then when Angelo stops for a moment one of the sisters says to Angelo, 'I hear that the people call you *Barani* now, do they think that you are their priest?' 'Barani' is used for both a priest and an honourable old man. Angelo laughs about it and says, 'Sister, what do people know? I am just a simple catechist.' I seldom disagree with Angelo, but now I am not so sure. Just a simple catechist, but I know from the story of his life that being a simple catechist is not so simple. This man addresses me as Barani and I let him, but since this morning I have joined the people and call him Barani Angelo. What do people know? I am inclined to think that people know a great deal.

DON'T BOAST

He who boasts much can do little.
Niger proverb

Moudie is his name. It means 'Don't boast', or 'Remain humble'. In many parts of Africa names play a peculiar role; people become what they are called. That is the case with Moudie and he is proud of the fact that he is not the boasting type, more of a humble man. He might be humble but that does not mean he is shy.

It is not very common here in Sudan for people to comment on the priest's homily. It is not common among the Azande that they comment or give compliments at all, at least not in the subject's presence. But this morning Moudie told me after Mass that he agreed with what I had said in the homily. Maybe Moudie did not intend to make a compliment but just wanted to state that he and I agreed. We had read Mark, chapter 8, where Christ tells his disciples about his impending suffering and death. Peter won't hear of it, but Christ tells him more or less, 'You devil, get behind me, accept that cross as I accept it!' As Christians we have to accept the cross, and I had said something along these lines. And Moudie, who should not boast, comes and tells me that he fully agrees with me. But then, he has had his portion of hardship and suffering in his little more than thirty years.

He was born in the early sixties, not far from the border of Zaïre. It was wartime in South Sudan, the time of the first civil war, the *Anya-nya*, in which Moudie's people played an important role. Because of that, the government persecuted them and many people had to flee. Before he was five years old, Moudie became a refugee in Zaïre. Yes, Moudie remembers how he and his mother lived in Camp Seven and that later he went to school in Camp Eight. He was taught French, but does not remember much of the language except *merci beaucoup*, thank you very much. After all, that goes along fairly well with being humble, and he is a grateful human being.

In 1973, after the Addis Ababa agreement, he returned to Sudan, the country about which his father had told him all these years. Luckily for him, a school was soon started not far from his home village. It had been difficult for Moudie to say goodbye to the school in Zaïre. From a very early age he had been very keen to learn. It is said here in Sudan, 'A human being without education is like an animal without a hide'. For his secondary education he travelled all the way to Juba. It was quite a distance from home, but he wanted to try his luck. He was hungry for a secondary education. Even today he tells his pupils, 'Knowledge is like a garden; if it is not cultivated it cannot be harvested'. But he was not the only one who was looking for schooling in Juba, and his marks from the bush school of his village meant very little in the admission procedure of the Comboni secondary school. He was not admitted to the boys' school, but there were evening classes in one of the secondary schools for girls, and Moudie attended. Few students of these classes passed the secondary examination, but Moudie was highly motivated and studied night and day. He passed the examination. No, Moudie is not proud of it; that would be against his name, but he explains to me that you have to make the most of the opportunities which come your way.

Moudie came home with a certificate of secondary education. He had struggled for it, but that did not mean that he would keep his riches to himself. He intended to share what he knew with the people in his village, Ezo. He wanted to become a teacher, but the government did not give him a job in a government school. There were too few schools in any case. At the request of the parents, Moudie started his own establishment, a 'self-help' school, he called it. You cannot wait for a government to help if it is quite clear that it is uninterested. One often gets the impression that the government wants to keep the people in the south ignorant. With another teacher, the help of the parents and a little help from the church, he got things going.

His efforts did not go unnoticed: an Irish missionary who visited his school and heard Moudie talk about education, about development and the role of the church, offered him a place in a course for teaching religion. Moudie accepted it gratefully. I got to know Moudie in 1988 when he had just completed that course. Yes, he had returned to his self-help school, but now he could also assist the catechists, many of whom had very little education. With them and the parents of the schoolchildren, he started to build a church in his village, and he would come and pester me for school equipment and seeds for the school gardens. He also wanted zinc sheets for the roof of the church. Moudie will tell you that the right approach for him is *integral development*, which means getting the necessary co-operation from the people for the growth of the community. Moudie does not make distinctions, as we often do, between what is a social, pastoral, economic or religious problem. He thinks that these distinctions are not real. He has become the leader of the village, and the people accept his leadership all the more readily because he does not boast about it.

In 1990 he saw the government troops routed by the SPLA. They passed his school, and many of the local people were fleeing too. On his way to the Central African Republic, one of the priests had stopped and told Moudie that the SPLA were coming, and that he had better run. But Moudie could not leave his school behind to be looted. Whilst others were fleeing, Moudie and some of the parents packed all the school equipment into boxes and with some of the boys carried them into the forest. He was still packing when the SPLA were only six kilometres away. Naturally, the teacher had heard about the SPLA soldiers' looting, but he also knew that they were unpaid. When Moudie tells me about it later, he points out that he is simply explaining the circumstances rather than justifying their actions.

When they arrived in Ezo, the SPLA found the village deserted. Moudie and his people were close by, hiding in the forest near the border of Zaïre. They listened and watched from a distance to see what was going to happen. Moudie was among the first who went to have a look at the newcomers openly and meet them. At first the liberation army impressed him. Moudie is small in stature and he had to look up to these tall Dinka people. But he tells me that their being taller did not mean they knew more. Moudie, in his humble way, acted as the spokesman for his people. Soon enough the SPLA had asked him to join the movement, but he had no intention of becoming a soldier. Even when they had said that with his education he would quickly be given stars to wear on his uniform, Moudie had declined the offer. He was not interested in those kinds of stars.

He had told the SPLA recruiters that he was willing to take part in the fight to liberate his people, but that he wanted to fight with his own weapon, and it was a forceful one. At mention of a weapon, the soldiers pricked up their ears. They all had heard how during the sixties, in the first civil war, the Azande made their own guns, heavy guns which could hardly be held by one person, but which could kill an elephant. They were curious to hear about the weapon of this little fellow. When Moudie saw that he had their attention, he gave a little lecture to the SPLA on the importance of education.

Did they not see that the government in Khartoum fought not only with bullets, but with many other weapons as well? Was depriving people in the south of education not a way of suppressing them? The government was only too happy that there were few schools in the area liberated by the SPLA. It was high time to fight back. His weapon of liberation was education. Moudie had talked without fear that day: he had not boasted about himself; he allowed that he was not a highly-qualified teacher. But they all knew that even an ant can harm an elephant.

The soldiers had listened to him and they knew that this small man spoke the truth. Many of them had very little education and their only recourse was to become soldiers. Though many young men were pressed into the armed forces of the SPLA, in the end the SPLA accepted that Moudie should reopen his school. When he brought back his school equipment from the forest they had demanded a share of it for the soldiers. The teacher was wise enough not to resist, and even suggested that one of his colleagues could give literacy classes to the soldiers.

Moudie started to visit other schools and, as most of the priests were still refugees in the Central African Republic, he also visited the neighbouring missions to train the catechists to lead prayer services. A few years ago he asked me for a bicycle. Seeing how much he travelled, I found his request for a bicycle very reasonable. But I wondered whether it would not make the soldiers jealous and get him into trouble as some catechists got into trouble when they tried to hold on to their bicycles? In the end he got his bicycle, and a few months later I inquired how things were going.

At times one has to suffer, Moudie told me. Yes, on one of his long journeys on his bicycle a Dinka soldier had stopped him. He had demanded the bicycle, pointing his gun and saying: 'I have walked all the way from the border of Ethiopia to liberate you. I have a right to that bicycle!' Moudie replied that he had never asked the Dinka to come and liberate him. In many ways he had liberated himself with his education. The soldier had become very angry and had threatened to shoot him. But if the bull threatens to throw you, it is better to lie down, and Moudie had been able to hold on to his life and his bicycle by agreeing to give the soldier a ride to the next village.

This was not the only time he had to suffer for sticking to his principles. He spent some days in prison, and he knows what it is to be caned. That was the time when he had not been willing to hand over all the copybooks which he had just received for his schools. He was willing to share what he received, but he had not been happy when he had been ordered to do so. He had said that he had a different commander from whom he took orders. The SPLA commander did not like that. Moudie adds, 'Maybe I was boasting that time, and you see what happens'. It is not always easy to find the right balance. It is true one should not boast too much, but he also knows the saying, 'a too-modest man will go hungry'.

Moudie has been staying with us the last few days. He has come to make arrangements for the transport of teak poles for the roof of a church which he has been building with his people. He also wants materials for the secondary school which he has started, very much against my advice. I have my doubts whether we can support two secondary schools in the diocese while this war continues. But Moudie keeps telling me that many young people want education and that we have to start this secondary school. He explains once more that it is not right that the young people must flee to Uganda in order to get an education. Moudie and I have argued a lot over the years, and at times I think that I am making life unnecessarily hard for him. I ask him whether he feels this way.

Moudie does not deny that he suffers because of some of my questioning, but my questioning also helps him to clarify his own ideas. But he adds that he does not believe in just avoiding suffering. That is exactly what he wanted to convey when he told me that he agreed with my homily that morning. For him suffering is part of life. If you are not willing to accept pain, you never will know joy. When you believe that the way Christ was going through life is a good way, you cannot pick only the nice parts, he tells me. If you take the stand that Christ took you are bound to get into difficulties; you even might be crucified. If you support those who are weak, it will be the brutes that are against you. If you do not participate in the corruption, then in the end you will have to face the cane. Moudie gives me a beautiful sermon about the value of the cross in the life of Christians. Some of the things he says would sound hollow if I said them, as I have not experienced the suffering that Moudie has gone through. Perhaps I should have asked Moudie to preach this morning. Even if Moudie means 'don't boast', I think I am proud of the fact that I am working with a man like him. Next time I will ask him to preach.

SISTER CLEMENTINA

*A silly daughter teaches her mother
how to bear children.*

Ethiopian proverb

Anne knew just enough of the art of baking bread to be able to explain it to Clementina, who was looking after the kitchen. Anne is a colleague of mine who, with her husband Frank, recently joined me to work in the Diocese of Tombura-Yambio. The local food is very good, and some people in Africa say, 'Follow the customs or flee the country'. We are not that radical and we think that it would be nice to have bread now and again. Bread is not a common commodity in South Sudan. The idea is welcomed not only by us Europeans, but by most of the African priests with whom we live in the bishop's house, and who got used to eating bread during their time in the seminary.

Anne had baked bread before, albeit with a different kind of yeast and a different oven, but she was confident enough to try. She explained it all to Clementina, who stood there looking on benevolently. To make sure, Anne had looked it all up in a cookery book and she hoped Clementina would be able to remember it all: so many cups of flour, so much yeast, so much water; you make a dough, and then you start kneading it. The kneading is important, and Anne was just getting the knack of it. Of course it was a bit messy, the dough sticking to hands and fingers. There Clementina nearly gave the game away, when she showed Anne how to get the stuff off her hands with a bit of dry flour. The first buns were not a great success, but they were edible. Anne explained to Clementina that she would try once more with a different amount of yeast and perhaps let the dough rise a bit longer. Maybe they could have another go at it tomorrow. And Clementina nodded, as Africans have nodded at Europeans for generations, and after that they go away and do things the way they know best.

When Anne left the kitchen, Clementina had started over, and she baked some beautiful loaves the way she had learned in Mupoi from the Italian sisters. That must have been in 1960, before Anne was born. Later, when Anne came into the kitchen and found that some flour was missing, she asked Clementina about it. Clementina had said, 'Leave it to me, I think I know who has taken it, but I have to check it out further.' It bothered Anne that things kept disappearing from the kitchen. She was glad that she could leave this to Clementina, who knew her own people.

We all had a good laugh about it when we sat down to eat that evening. We looked at the *bakinde*, a sorghum dish, which was left over from the afternoon. It is good food but to eat it three times a day is a bit much. Frank tried to get a rise out of Anne about her bread-baking, and Anne said that she and Clementina would try again tomorrow. At that point, Clementina, standing in the doorway, asked Frank whether he had any margarine. Frank wanted to tease Anne some more about the lack of bread, and went to the cupboard to get some margarine to put on the bread that he didn't have, only to discover two beautiful loaves. We knew that only Clementina could have baked them. We all had a good laugh, and although we did not know how she had done it, we applauded Clementina. Clementina smiled and went back to the kitchen. Of course Anne felt a bit silly, like the daughter who teaches her mother to bear children. But from that moment on she was willing to see Clementina as her teacher. Certainly Clementina could teach us all plenty.

Some weeks earlier, we had needed somebody to look after the kitchen in the bishop's house and to supervise the cleaning. One of the priests had suggested that we ask Sister Clementina. She was a widow looking for work and the fact that she spoke good English was a great advantage for us who knew hardly anything of the local language. Clementina came to introduce herself, dressed in white, a sign of mourning for her husband who had died a few months before. The life of a widow is not easy in Azande culture, as in many other African cultures. After the funeral of her husband everything is taken away from her, even her clothes. Dressed only in a grass skirt and covered with leaves she is sent back to her family. For Clementina it had not been so clear where her family was. She did not have many relatives, and those she had were far away. Clementina had thought about it, and in the end she had decided to go to the church. After all, in some way that was her home. After listening to her, the parish priest had accepted her and he had given her a hut in the church compound.

For Clementina it was a sort of homecoming. Her father had grown up as an orphan in Mupoi, the first mission station in this area, built by the Comboni missionaries. It was a small town in the middle of the jungle of South Sudan. It could have been a small town in Italy, the brothers who built most of it being Italian. Here they fired their own bricks and tiles; they had their own carpentry shop and sawmill. They even planted vines and made their own wine. Mupoi became a major religious and social centre. It also boasted a primary and secondary school, training for religious brothers and sisters. Here Clementina's father grew up and here she was born, over fifty years ago. She was still very young when her father died. Her father had been a Christian, but this did not mean that the traditional customs had not to be followed. Clementina's mother was sent home to her relatives, naked, without even her children. Before the father died he had put on paper that he willed Clementina and her brothers and sisters to the church, because for him, an orphan, the church had become his clan. He was confident that in this way his children would be well looked after as he had been well looked after in Mupoi mission.

Clementina missed her mother a lot, but apart from that she did not have a bad life. She went to school, which at that time was still fairly exceptional for girls. When she was thirteen she became an aspirant to join the sisters. She was among the first of the African candidates. When I asked her why she wanted to be a sister, Clementina answered, 'I think I wanted to serve God by serving our people. I did not have a special reason, and I think that there are no good reasons why one joins the sisters nor why one becomes a priest'. During her training Clementina learned the things which a sister in training learned in Italy, including baking bread. For part of her education she was sent to Uganda. She was trained to become a teacher, not because she wanted to be one particularly, but because the missionaries needed African teachers for the education of girls. 'We always obeyed', Clementina says with a smile.

But then, in the early sixties, the civil war began. The government accused the missionaries of supporting the rebels. This has never been demonstrated, but it would be worse if it could be shown that they were *not* on the side of the people of South Sudan, among whom they were working. Then all the missionaries were told to leave the country in 1964. Clementina was in Mboki, near Tombura, at that time. She remembers how upset the missionaries had been. The Italian Apostolic Vicar of Mupoi had called all the African sisters together. He had told them, more or less, that the Italian sisters and he had come to the conclusion that the African sisters could hardly remain sisters without them, and that they were released from their vows and could go home. This had upset the African sisters. Some of the sisters took the Apostolic Vicar at his word and had gone back to their villages, but to Clementina and a few others it did not make sense. They had not become sisters to serve the missionaries, but the church and its people. They knew that the church was not leaving with the missionaries. They decided to remain sisters and see where it would lead them. Soon enough they realized that they could not keep up all the big buildings, but they did what they could for and with the people.

But the war in the south broadened, and it was no longer safe to stay in Mupoi or in Mboki. The African priests and sisters fled with their people to the Central

African Republic and Zaïre, leaving the mission buildings to be invaded by the army and the forest, and to turn to ruins. But in spite of everything, the church grew among the people in exile. Some of the sisters remained together and lived the religious life, and though they adhered to many Italian rituals, gradually African ways entered their lives: they cultivated their own gardens, and became more open to relatives and their needs than they had been under the missionaries.

In 1973 the African sisters returned to Sudan. The new bishop, Joseph Gasi Abangite, welcomed them back to Mupoi. Rome had suggested that the few African sisters of different congregations who had survived the exile, form one new congregation. This was not easy, but an effort was made. However, plans which are made in Rome do not always work in Africa. Clementina went back to Uganda to be trained as a midwife; that is what she had originally wanted to be. When she returned to Mupoi there was considerable tension in the convent. Some sisters had secondary education; others had hardly finished primary school; there were financial problems; there was tension between sisters who had previously belonged to different congregations. For Clementina it was not any longer a peaceful life in the convent. She does not go into details, but says the new congregation was no longer serving the church by serving the people. She left the convent without very well-defined reasons. But then she did not have good reasons for entering in the first place.

It was no problem for Clementina to find work. There were not many women around with a good education. She could have started teaching again, but the nursing profession appealed more. For many years Clementina was a midwife. She assisted women in bringing children into the world, knowing that she herself would never have children. It had taken some courage to tell the man who wanted to marry her that she would not be able to have children. But this policeman, who had a few children already with another woman, had proposed to her all the same. The fact that Clementina could not have children of her own did not mean that she was ever without children in her home. She adopted the child of a niece of hers, who had sleeping sickness, and relatives regularly sent children to Aunt Clementina, knowing that she would look after them.

Not to speak ill of the dead, but with a great sigh Clementina admits that she did not have a wonderful marriage. No, her husband was not a bad man, but he drank a lot and his drinking brought problems. Perhaps it was the other way round and his problems drove him to drink. Clementina does not know, but she knows that her husband had a very difficult job. To be a policeman for a government which suppresses your own people is not easy. But Clementina looked after him. In the end she accepted him as another difficult child.

Clementina worked in the hospital in Yambio during the time that I was a regular visitor there. She knew me long before I knew her. When I fled in 1990 after the SPLA announced they were on their way, Clementina remained in Yambio. When the government troops were routed, many people fled to Zaïre and the Central African Republic. Clementina had seen it all before, and decided not to run this time. She withdrew with her husband and the children into the forest where they built a hut, not far from Gangura, a small village on the road to Zaïre. After the arrival of the SPLA, Clementina's husband did not go back to work. He did not know how acceptable a government policeman would be to these liberators. Soon he heard that they were recruiting soldiers, but he did not want to fight. He withdrew further into the forest and drank himself to death. With her children helping, Clementina started to clear the land. She planted fields with cassava, groundnuts and sorghum, the traditional crops. Then when the people of World Vision arrived with vegetable seeds, she put in onions, tomatoes and cabbages too. The people of World Vision discovered her in the forest when they started a small clinic in Gangura.

They asked her to work in their clinic and Clementina accepted the offer. From the nurses of World Vision I hear that Clementina was probably the most dedicated nurse they had seen for a long time. As a nurse she was addressed as 'Sister' again and she was content serving her community once more as a sister. She was at work in the clinic on the day she heard that her husband had fallen sick. She ran home at once, and with the help of neighbours brought him to the hospital in Yambio. The services there are not very good, or perhaps she had got her husband there too late. Clementina does not blame anybody, but a few days later he died.

After the funeral Clementina was sent 'home' with nothing. She had to leave her hut, was not even allowed to harvest the groundnuts in her own field. According to her tradition she had to leave it all behind. African tradition can be very cruel. Where could she go? As a child, when her father died she had been given to the church. She sought out the nearest Catholic church and that is how she arrived at the church in Yambio.

When the people of World Vision discovered where she had gone, they came to ask her to return and work in the clinic. But Clementina declined. She just wanted the simple life of service, which she had known as a young sister. She accepted work in the bishop's house, to see to it that everything is kept clean, to supervise the kitchen, and to train the few missionaries who live there, even if it meant teaching them how to bake bread.

DISPLACED AT HOME

He who runs from the white ant,
may stumble upon the stinging ant.

Nigerian proverb

I had just started to work with the New Sudan Council of Churches in 1991, when the civil war in Ethiopia came to an end. It was a great blessing for Ethiopia, but it was a blow to the SPLA in the south of Sudan, because for years the Liberation Army had been supplied with weapons via Ethiopia, and many SPLA soldiers had received their training there. But above all, many southern Sudanese who had fled from the war had established themselves in the Ethiopian refugee camps, of which Itang, Pinyudo and Dima are the best known. In Itang alone more than 300,000 Sudanese had found a temporary home. They received food from the UNHCR, there were schools for the children, there was medical care, and they had been able to start growing their own crops. In the camps, the refugees had been relatively safe from the bombardments of the Sudanese government, which was hesitant to fly into Ethiopia.

Being a refugee in a foreign land is difficult, but often it is better than being displaced in one's own country. Moreover, in some parts of Africa it is often hard to say what 'one's own country' means, for the borders were drawn in colonial days, with scant regard for tribal boundaries. Nowadays many tribes occupy both sides of a national border. Which is their country, the tribal home with borders undelineated on maps, or the borders of the present-day country? It is hard to say. One thing is sure;

often tribal allegiance is far stronger than national ties. Not everybody will accept that this is so; western countries cling to the borders which they drew in the past, which certainly makes things simpler for the UNHCR, but not for the people in Sudan.

Now under the new regime in Ethiopia, the refugees, rightly or wrongly, no longer felt welcome. Through the years, they have had to flee war several times. It is said, 'Wood already touched by fire is not hard to set alight.'[1] The people of the camps returned to Sudan, although they knew that the situation there was far from peaceful. Within a few days of the new Ethiopian regime, over a quarter of a million people crossed the border near Nasir. The world press did not cover this tragic migration, as it would later report the flight of the people of Rwanda, for the simple reason that journalists could not reach the area.

Difficult access was a problem not only for the press, but for all the non-governmental organizations and aid agencies, representatives of which gathered in the readily-accessible Kenyan capital, Nairobi, to see what could be done for the returning Sudanese. I attended that meeting as a representative of the still wet-behind-the-ears New Sudan Council of Churches. Since the Sudanese were back in their own country, they were no longer the responsibility of the United Nations: technically, they were not refugees but people displaced within their own country. As such they were left to the care of NGOs and the churches.

It was a tedious meeting. Of course it is very important that this kind of relief work is properly co-ordinated, but relief work suffers from having taken on the characteristics of a giant industry. There is competition: at times it seemed as if organizations were fighting with each other over who would get the biggest piece of the cake of misery in the southern Sudan. The group of over 10,000 unaccompanied minors was a particular bone of contention. Every organization wanted to look after them. These young boys, who had gone to Ethiopia for their education, would be prime fund-raising material for any

---

[1] This is a proverb of the Ashanti people in West Africa.

NGO or aid organization. I listened, knowing that our young Council of Churches had no plane and little cash, and reaching Nasir and Pochalla, the points where the refugees crossed into Sudan, required the small planes of the Red Cross or the UN. Both organizations were over-loaded with requests for cargo space, and they were also carrying their own supplies. Flying for the churches certainly was not a priority for them. Tired and disap-pointed that we could not offer help, I returned to my base in Torit.

Bishop Paride Taban, then the chairman of the NSCC, betrayed astonishment that I had come home so soon. I reported my experience of the meeting in Nairobi, and said that I had concluded we were too small to make a significant contribution. Other organizations seemed extremely, overly keen, so let them get on with it. Anyway, what could we share with the returning refugees? We had nothing. The bishop listened to all this and was quiet for a while. Then he said, 'My friend', (he usually calls me Mathew, but when he disagrees with me he addresses me as 'friend'), 'Your reasoning is wrong; you are not working for one or other foreign NGO, you are working for the Sudanese churches. The people who are returning to Sudan are our *own* people, our own brothers and sisters. How can you relinquish responsibility for them to foreign NGOs?' Unconvinced, I reiterated that we had next to nothing to offer. Moreover, I myself was a foreigner. But Bishop Paride insisted that solidarity means more than emergency relief or material help.

An hour later I am on the radio requesting the UN to reserve two places for tomorrow's flight to Nasir. Bishop Taban is highly respected at the UN, and I doubt I would have been able to get a place without him. The next day we land in the United Nations' Twin Otter on the morass of an airstrip at Nasir. The mud flies higher than the wings of the plane, but the Ethiopian pilot is confident that he can take off again, since the airstrip is being reinforced with bricks from the ruins of the town. SPLA commanders, Riek Machar and Lam Akol turn out to welcome us; prob-ably they have heard that Bishop Taban is on the plane. After the bombardment, very few buildings remain standing; it has been raining for the last few days, and Nasir is a mud-hole. At the UN camp we are supplied with gumboots. But even with these it is difficult to walk through the muddy soil. A few days ago more than 150,000 returning Sudanese were registered here. They have settled for the time being in and around the churches and schools. The local Nuer people have also offered them their big cattle barns, and have shared their food with them. They have even slaughtered cows for their displaced compatriots; cows are the most precious possession of the Nuer, and they don't part with them easily. But even traditional African hospitality has its limits. Now there is little food left. In this area of Sudan grows a species of grass which, at a pinch can nourish humans, but even this grass cannot be found any more.

We travel by boat from one settlement of displaced people to the next, and see corpses floating in Sobat River. Many are the corpses of children, 'Too weak to make it across the river', murmurs one of our guides. As we arrive in Pandanyang, a throng of boys pulls our boat on to the bank. They do not hide their disappointment when they see that we have brought no food. This is a settlement of over 5,000 boys and a few teachers. The boys, aged between eight and fifteen, gather around us. The younger ones cling to us and beg for food. The UN has been able to fly in some biscuits, but yesterday five children died, and one child died as we are there. I feel helpless and I think it would have been better to put some food on the plane instead of me.

I am not the only one who feels helpless to save these lives. In the UN camp, where most relief workers are staying, there is an atmosphere of frustrated powerlessness. To watch people die without being able to do something is impossible to bear. A few days ago a Hercules transport dropped about ten tons of military food rations left over from the Gulf War. What is the use of Nescafé or nutritionless powdered potatoes for people who are dying of starvation? A shipment of fishing-nets has arrived, which is a step in the right direction, but most organizations are still scratching around for funds.

In the evening we gather with other relief workers in the camp. They ask Bishop Taban to go to Nairobi and explain to the world how serious, and also how unjust, the situation is. We sit here in Nasir, a few kilometres from the Ethiopian border. The Nuer people live on both sides of this border. In Ethiopia these people had the status of refugees and were cared for by the UNHCR. Now they and many of the local people are completely dependent on charity. They cannot travel on from here during the rainy season; the swamps cannot be crossed. It will take six months before they can reach their home regions, and in any case some of these areas are definitely not safe to return to. In Sudan, time and time again we are confronted with the sharp distinction made by officials between the internal and external refugees. More than half a million people are displaced within Sudan and they have no official status whatsoever. The local population here has made a great effort to welcome those returning, but they now have hardly any food left themselves. We spend a sleepless night in our tent with many mosquitoes.

Next morning we get on a plane which has brought medicines. One of the relief workers wonders: 'What medicine is there against hunger?' The pilot tries to take off but has to abort as he cannot get up enough speed in the mud. We laugh about it and remain calm, as the pilot remains calm and seems confident that he can get us out of the mud. He turns round and the second time he manages to get into the air just before running out of airstrip. Soon enough the pilot tells us that he is getting ready to land again in Pochalla, a few hundred kilometres south of Nasir.

Pochalla consists of a few brick buildings and a broken pump from the colonial days. The small river makes the border with Ethiopia. Until last week Pochalla was the home of a hundred families and millions of mosquitoes.

When we land, thousands of boys come running to the airstrip. They are living under the trees, having marched here from Pinyudo in Ethiopia. They are not malnourished yet, and with the help of their leaders they have started their own gardens. Some are assigned to search for edible fruits and berries, others sit with their copy-

books under the trees and try to get on with their inter-
rupted education. Their leaders appear to be a cross of
soldier and teacher; they tell us how they had to run
when their camp in Pinyudo was attacked by the soldiers
of OLF (Oromo Liberation Front) and troops of the
Khartoum government. They had organized the evacua-
tion of the children first, and had arrived here with about
10,000 of them. They had been bombed along the way;
though the bombing was inaccurate and there were no
casualties, it had scared the life out of the children. The
soldier-teachers inform us that another 86,000 people are
on their way to Pochalla and that probably they will arrive
here tomorrow. A few people of the International Red
Cross have managed to get here before us and they have
set up a small camp where we are allowed to put up our
tents. The Red Cross workers have come to see what they
can do for the returnees, but they do not have the funds
or aircraft to start a big relief operation. They estimate
that 400,000 Sudanese refugees will return to Sudan from
Ethiopia.

At the first signs of darkness the millions of mosquitoes
descend and we dive into our tents. We have not eaten all
day. Almost secretly we eat a sandwich which we have
brought from Nasir. It is not easy to eat when thousands
of hungry children are watching you. The plane, which
brought us, has flown on to Lokichokio on the border of
Kenya and Sudan. We will be picked up the day after
tomorrow by another plane returning from Nasir. Without
much discussion, it is clear to us that as representatives of
the churches we should be here tomorrow to welcome
the 86,000 returnees who are now on their way to
Pochalla. After that we cannot go home to Torit, but we
will go on to Nairobi where we will approach partner
churches in America and Europe to see how we can
support all these people who are refugees in their own
country. I fully agree now with the bishop that we cannot
leave this work to foreign NGOs. I fall asleep while ten
thousand boys sing warrior songs, fighting off the mosquitoes around them.

When we get up next morning we hear that the first
wave of returnees are crossing the border river. More

than 50,000 people – the figures change daily – are on the way, and we have nothing to offer them. I feel far from comfortable. However, the bishop seems to be energized when he hears people have started to arrive. He washes his face, puts on a black shirt with Roman collar and his bishop's cross, and together we walk to the river. He welcomes the first arrivals as he pulls them up the bank on to the Sudanese side. Then the great river of people starts arriving. They carry their belongings on their heads. Some have brought their cattle with them, a cow or a few goats, but nothing like the great herds which they once owned. Many carry some food, anticipating that they will not find much here.

Together with the bishop I stand on some stepping-stones in the river and for hours we just shake hands with people. We don't even know the language of most of them. I bid them welcome in English, but I might as well have said it in Dutch. Some people of Eastern Equatoria recognize Bishop Paride and they laugh together in greeting. Others have tears in their eyes when they enter their own country again. On the bank a few people of the International Red Cross are counting the returnees. They tell us that more than 3,000 people are now crossing the river every hour. I wonder whether they consider all this shaking of hands a waste of time, or is each one of us doing what we know best? The Europeans are planning, and the Africans are building relations; both, of course, will be needed to support these people who are returning to Sudan. Many have been refugees since the start of the war in 1983. Most seem happy to be returning, but they do not know what lies ahead. Even the great Red Cross has nothing to offer yet except a little medicine in the clinic, which they opened a few days ago.

Yes, I worry about where we can get food for these people. What can we as churches do for them? It does not seem to trouble my friend, Paride, who still stands in the river shaking thousands of hands. Slowly I become aware that I am learning something in this river. We Europeans are generous, we cultivate generosity, but when we must, we often find it difficult to go to people empty-handed. Do I feel uneasy today because we have nothing to share except ourselves? Maybe the only thing we are doing here is letting these people know that they are not forgotten. I have not kept it up as long as Bishop Paride Taban there in the river, but it is important that he stands there. I wonder whether we can allow ourselves to share what we have, our material things, if we are not prepared to share *who* we are.

A small planeload of journalists arrives, flown in by the UN. Their coming is important, for journalists are often the eyes of the world and it is essential that the nations should know what is happening here. So often the war victims in the Sudan are forgotten. Tired, the bishop returns from the river and the journalists descend on him like so many mosquitoes. But he has told me before the mosquitoes leave you alone once you give them their fill of your blood, sooner than if you keep chasing them away.

They fire their questions. They want to know the statistics. What is the UN doing? Why has the Red Cross not flown in any food? All these boys here, the so-called unaccompanied minors, are they indeed boys in search of education or are they child soldiers? And so it goes on.

Then there again is the question which has been with us all these days: whose responsibility is it really, to look after all these people?

The bishop avoids answering some of the questions but he is willing to answer this one. 'These people are Sudanese. Some organizations are inclined to claim these boys as their own. Let them remember that we don't give away our children. These people are victims of the war. The war itself, the starving people, the displacement of people, the division of people, all the pain and suffering is the cross we have to bear. No, we don't reject the cross. We are not asking the world to take the cross away from us. We are willing to carry our cross. But even Christ did not carry his cross alone: Simon of Cyrene helped him part of the way. We are not asking the world to carry our cross; we are only asking them to be our Simon of Cyrene.'

SOLIDARITY

*A cow gave birth to fire: she wanted to lick
it, but it burned; she wanted to leave it, but
she could not because it was her own child.*

Ethiopian proverb

The organization called Pax Christi wrote a good report
about the situation in Sudan: *A Cry For Peace*. This report
caused some commotion in Sudanese government circles,
as it was very critical of the fundamentalist government in
Khartoum. The hurried fact-finding visit of the delegation
of Pax Christi at the end of 1993 had been fruitful, at least
in some respects. The report clearly pointed out the
suffering of the people in Sudan, the violations of human
rights, and it expressed its solidarity with the people. Few
Sudanese would be able to read *A Cry For Peace*, but Pax
Christi wanted to express its solidarity with these people,
a solidarity which certainly had not been accomplished by
the flying visit of the delegation.

Following this first visit of Pax Christi, I visited the
churches in Leer, in Upper Nile Province. For a long time
this area had been quite isolated on account of the war,
and the fact that it cannot be reached by road. A few
months earlier a Comboni missionary had visited the area,
but otherwise no priest had been there since the beginning of the civil war in 1983. I received a warm welcome
from the Catholics, but no less from the Presbyterians.
These churches were very much alive and were growing
now as they had never grown before. Proudly the people
showed me how they were building a church and a house
for a priest in the hope that soon one would come to
serve them. When they heard that I was a Mill Hill

missionary they came with stories about colleagues of mine whom they had known before 1964. I celebrated the Eucharist with them and they sang it in Latin, as was customary in the fifties.

Yes, I was very welcome, but when we sat in the evening under the stars people also started to express their disappointments. They felt that they had been deserted by what they call their 'mother churches'. The bishop of Malakal could not visit this area, the town where he lives being still in government hands. Many of the people here, strong supporters of the SPLA, felt that their bishop should join them. I know that things are never as simple as they appear, but it is reasonable that these people should feel disappointed. They ask basic, penetrating questions: Why have the churches in Europe, who sent the first missionaries, forgotten them? Which bishop, which church leader has visited them in these difficult times? Why have my colleagues, who baptized them long ago, not come to see them? I tell them that most of the Mill Hill missionaries, whom they recall, died long ago. But a few old catechists are overjoyed when they hear that Father Spakauskas is still alive, and they recite the *Confiteor* in Latin for me, which he had taught them. Then the questions continue. Why did the Pope visit Khartoum, the town of the oppressor, and not the south of Sudan where the Christians live? It is no use trying to explain that the Pope had to follow diplomatic channels, and that the government never would have given him permission to visit Leer. Not everybody agrees that the Pope should have gone to Khartoum if he was not allowed to visit the south. They may be right, though the Christians in the north saw his visit as a sign of great solidarity. I listened to it all, not knowing what to answer. In some ways these people were right and even where they were not right I could sympathize with their feelings.

In the colonial days, this area was evangelized by American Presbyterians, and there had been very little co-operation between Presbyterian and Catholic missionaries. There are many Catholics in this area now, and the two churches co-operate very well. They have an inter-church committee that organizes all sorts of activities, from cattle vaccinations to making mosquito netting. The churches have certainly influenced each other: the Catholics have a Presbyterian slant and though the Presbyterians might not pray the rosary, several of them wear one around their necks. However, this co-operation is not always easy and the difference of denomination can divide families. I remember we had a long discussion about whether the Catholic catechist had the right to baptize the mother of the Presbyterian evangelist. As a member of the NSCC I work with both churches and I often feel that the differences between these churches have very little to do with life in the Upper Nile Province. We missionaries brought a divided Christianity to Africa and it has not been a blessing. Such were my thoughts and impressions on my first trip to Leer.

Back in Nairobi, I heard that the chairman of Pax Christi, Cardinal Danneels of Belgium, was willing to come and visit South Sudan. I was asked to organize his journey. After I shared my experience of the disappointment in Leer with some of the church leaders, they fully agreed that it would be a good place for his visit. True, Cardinal Danneels is not the Pope, but he might become one in future. Not being the Pope, who is dependent on diplomatic channels, the chairman of Pax Christi would be free to visit South Sudan and express solidarity with the church there. Yes, Leer would be an excellent place to include in the itinerary. It was suggested that the delegation should go on to visit Nimule, where Bishop Paride Taban had made his temporary home on fleeing Torit after the government take-over in 1992. Near Nimule was one of the huge camps for the displaced people in Aswa. Most of those displaced were Christians and the presence of a western church leader would be greatly appreciated.

It was not too difficult to plan this visit, though not everybody was happy that the cardinal would be the guest of the churches. He was not only an important church leader but also an important Belgian, and the Belgian embassy was claiming him. The UN also thought that Danneels was important enough to have in their sphere, but then the UN must take instructions from Khartoum, and that would restrict the cardinal's movements.

It was still very early when two small planes left Nairobi airport. One plane carried the delegation of Pax Christi and the chairman of the New Sudan Council of Churches, Bishop Paride Taban, as the host. The other plane was filled with journalists, especially from Holland and Belgium. The small plane could carry only eight of them and their equipment, but the journalists had agreed to pool the TV cameraman in order to save money, and also to give another journalist a chance of coming along.

At dawn we had breakfast in Lokichokio, in the camp of the company from which we had chartered our planes. The Pax Christi delegation and the journalists had a chance to get to know each other. It was a group sympa-thetic with the situation in Sudan and the journalists were looking for the best way to express their solidarity. They agreed that whatever they published should be supportive of the Sudanese. The areas which we were going to visit were under the control of the SPLA, which welcomed the visit, and had informed us a few days ago that they could guarantee our security. But they had added that they could not shield us from bombardment by the government. Of course, even without us informing them, the government would know about this trip. The government always seems to know. But then nobody in South Sudan could be shielded from the bombardments by the government.

For nearly three hours we flew into the Sudan, first over the hills, then the great plains, till we saw under us the Sudd, the largest swamp in the world. Soon we were circling over Leer. From the plane we could see that the airstrip was black with people. The plane with journalists landed first in order to film the cardinal's landing. When his plane came to a standstill, the people sang and danced around it. Through a loudspeaker connected to a car battery, 'Cardinal Daniel' was welcomed. Danneels is such an un-African name, and the cardinal did not seem to mind that he had been suddenly baptized Daniel, or perhaps he did not notice.

Surrounded by thousands of singing and dancing people, we are led to a compound next to the airstrip. In the last few days the people have built their own cathedral here for this special occasion: a huge fence of grass, and a sanctuary shaded by a roof of plastic bags which had once contained relief food. On each sack is written in bold: *A gift from the American people.* In the centre of the grass cathedral there is a small altar table and chairs for the celebrants and some of the visitors. The thousands of people sit in the open, under the already scorching sun. New groups are arriving, each with its own drum and flag. Some have marched for days in order to be present at this celebration.

This is just the third time in ten years that the Eucharist has been celebrated here. Not only Catholics participate, but also the Presbyterians and the people who have held on to their traditional religion. At least 5,000 people are present. The choirs of the different churches, usually rivals, have practised together. Some melodies are Catholic in origin, others are American Presbyterian, but the ones that are sung with the most soul are the Nuer songs which have grown over the last ten years, songs with roots in the Bible and this endless war. These are known by all; in some way they not only sing these songs but they live them.

The cardinal's homily is full of astonishment and admiration for the church here, so full of life in spite of the war, and in spite of many years' isolation. Now he realizes that the real cathedrals are not built of bricks, but of people, he tells his audience. He offers no empty promises of all manner of material help. Pax Christi only seeks to be a voice for those who have no advocate. The people applaud, and they sing the liturgy. Five thousand wish each other peace, all the while singing and dancing together. They wish each other the peace which one day must be possible, even here in Sudan. Journalists busy with their cameras, sweat pouring down their faces, try to catch all that is happening.

Then the cardinal, the bishop and the visitors are asked to sit down and listen to what the people have to say. Their leaders tell us about the war; they talk about their churches, they ask that either priests be sent to them or that some of their catechists be ordained. They have more questions than the cardinal or anybody else can possibly answer. But their main request to Pax Christi is to let the world know what is happening in southern Sudan. One of the people says: 'At times we are jealous of the people in Bosnia; there people die, but they die before the cameras of the world and the world knows about them, takes notice and tries to do something about it. Here in South Sudan people die like people in Bosnia, but nobody knows, and nobody seems to care. It is as if the people die for nothing.'

One of the pilots of the planes comes and informs us that the UN is telling them over the radio not to fly on to Nimule as they cannot guarantee our safety. Possibly the UN is under pressure from Khartoum. We discuss it. It is obvious that the people in Nimule never would understand that we did not visit them just because Khartoum did not wish it. The owners of the plane discuss the situation over the radio with the SPLA in Nimule, and again the assurance is, 'Apart from bombardment from Khartoum, we guarantee that it is safe to visit Nimule and Aswa'. The people with whom we want to express solidarity are always in danger of being bombarded; our presence will not endanger them further. It is late afternoon when we land in Nimule and the pilots take off again quickly; they must make it back to Lokichokio before dark. They do not like to leave their planes in Sudan overnight.

We spend the night in Nimule on the border of Uganda, where the Nile enters Sudan. The journalists interview people till late in the night. When we sit in the dark under the stars they wonder how safe they are here. Some think that their presence might prevent the government from bombing civilians. Others, especially a few Sudanese, are inclined to think the opposite. One thing is sure; the government does not bomb at night. Everybody is tired and we sleep in peace.

Next morning we all leave by car to go to Aswa, where 80,000 displaced people are encamped. They have been moved from one place to the next, on the run from the government troops. Many of their brothers and sisters have moved across the border into Uganda. Those remaining are struggling to survive in their own country. Yes, they have been provided with some food aid but, expecting that thcy might be here for a long time, they have started their own gardens too. There is a school for the children, but not enough room for everybody. Nobody knows how long they can stay here; the war is very close. Pageri, a town close by, was bombed a few days ago. These people of Aswa have not much of a future here, indeed to us the situation looks hopeless.

But today they are putting on a festival to celebrate our visit. The Dinkas sing their many biblical songs, born during this war, songs of deep faith and courage. There are speeches of welcome and visits to the hospital and schools. Then there are the traditional dances. There is a moment of uneasiness when a group of war victims, with one leg or no legs but crutches, start to dance. Despite their mutilation they dance well. The visitors hardly dare to remark the irony of this, but they join in the laughter when they see that all the people around them laugh and applaud.

Then the leaders sit down with us for the more serious talks. We talk about solidarity. It has very little to do with giving food. The same nations that provide food for the displaced provide the weapons used in this war. One church leader explains that solidarity is not just about food, material or money, however important these things may be; it has more to do with human hands, warm hands with which we reach out to each other. This visit, though very short and improvised, is an effort to reach out to each other. Then saying our goodbyes and again shaking many hands, we make our way back to the airstrip in Nimule, where the two small planes are waiting to take us to Nairobi. That same evening the cardinal has to fly back to Brussels.

We wave him off at the airport. Tired, but relieved that everything went well, we return home. So often I have doubts about some of the programmes and projects we are involved in. It is not always easy to know the right thing to do. But that evening I felt confident that we had done the right thing in organizing this visit of Pax Christi. I went to bed grateful for the fact that next day I could sleep in and have a day of rest.

It was a rude awakening next morning when one of my

colleagues knocked on my door to tell me that Aswa had been bombed in the early hours. Seven people had been killed and many were wounded. Was this the government's retaliation for our visit of solidarity? Was this danger already there yesterday, and was that the reason why the UN had asked us not to go? How many people would have died if the bombing had taken place yesterday when thousands of people were gathered in that place? That same afternoon the cardinal faxed a message of sympathy and solidarity. We never will have answers to our questions: the Sudan government would never admit to bombing Aswa, let alone tell us why.

MISSIONARIES IN TENTS

You can tell good millet only after the harvesting.
Kenyan proverb

We sit on the rock in front of the chapel tent. The sisters have spread a few mats on this massive outcropping of black granite. The moon shines through the branches of the biggest fig tree that I have ever seen. There are drums in the distance but it is very peaceful here. About 150 metres away from us, the girls of the boarding school begin to sing their evening prayer before they go to bed. The sisters and I have also just prayed some psalms by the light of the moon and a cheap kerosene lamp. We said our prayers here on the rock as it is still rather hot in the chapel tent. We are drinking sweet tea as we talk, somewhat light-heartedly, about what it means for us to be missionaries.

Sister Lwanga thinks that mission mainly consists in sharing the Good News, and she backs her argument with the Bible, quoting John 1.35–51, where Jesus called his first apostles and sends them on their way. But from the stories of Sister Martha about her youth in Uganda, it is quite clear that at times missionaries have been bad news. She tells of missionaries who had scant respect for the very valuable traditions of her clan and tribe. They brought their own traditions with them, ignoring that the Ugandans had their own established ways. 'Some even thought that they had to bring God to Africa. They did not realize that God was there long before they arrived.'

I have heard these stories before, and in some ways I

have been part of the syndrome. But here we are looking for better ways. I suggest that mission can also be seen as a dialogue where we share together, where we are sent to each other and share who we are. We can leave it open, who gets converted by whom; maybe in the sharing both parties are converted. Sister Martha, who is in a bit of a provocative mood tonight, remarks that nobody is harder to convert than a missionary. If that missionary is a priest then it is even harder, she thinks. When you are a priest, or a sister for that matter, you are in a position of power in the church. She wonders whether dialogue is possible without equality. She even thinks that people are more open to each other when in some ways they are powerless.

Sister Josephine, who prefers crochet work to engaging in abstract discussions, says that she leaves it all to the Holy Spirit. 'The Spirit can sort it out. After all, mission is the work of the Spirit,' somebody had told her. She had liked that; it meant one worry less for her. She adds that it is all right to give the Holy Spirit a helping hand, but we should not try to take the lead. We laugh about it: four missionaries on a rock in the moonlight, unsure what their lives are really about. Sister Lwanga comes back to what Josephine said about the Spirit. We know that we should be open to that Spirit but we don't know where the Spirit will lead us. It is clear enough from the sisters' own lives as missionaries in Sudan.

'Missionary Sisters of Mary, Mother of the Church': that is their official name, but it is too involved for everyday life in Sudan, so they are called 'The Ugandan Sisters': it is short and everybody knows whom is meant. Uganda is the country where they were founded. It probably all started when the Pope visited Uganda in 1969. He had a lot to say to the African church. One of the things that stuck with Bishop Asili of Lira was that the Pope said the time had come for Africans to be missionaries to Africa. It is true that the great missionary, Comboni, had also said something like that, more than a hundred years earlier, but at that time Bishop Asili had not been around. The missionaries whom Bishop Asili knew were religious men or women who belonged to one or other foreign missionary order or congregation. To him it was plain that the Pope had asked Africans to start their own missionary congregations and that had been the beginning of the Missionary Sisters of Mary, Mother of the Church. The sisters are proud of the fact that they are missionaries. When Bishop Paride Taban had asked for some sisters to come to his diocese, they had gladly accepted his call. Sudan, a country where there are few missionaries, a country at war, a country where the people of the south are oppressed, certainly could be considered mission territory. That is how Sisters Lwanga, Martha and Josephine had found their way to the diocese of Torit, in the south of Sudan, bordering Uganda.

When they arrived in Torit, the town had already been liberated by the SPLA. With the bishop and his council they looked around for where their help was needed and wanted. The SPLA was trying to start a few schools and they welcomed any assistance, which the church could give. There also was a great shortage of medical personnel. So it was decided that Sister Lwanga and Sister Martha would start a school for girls in Torit. Sister Josephine accepted work in the hospital, which was run by the SPLA, with some assistance from Norwegian Church Aid. It was all part of an effort to assist the people of Torit to rebuild their lives in the liberated area of Sudan. People were happy that there was hope again.

However, the government in Khartoum was not at all happy that it had lost Torit to the SPLA. The Russian-built Antonov bomber flew over regularly and occasionally dropped some bombs around the town. It was terrifying, and we dug shelters next to our houses. Trenches were dug next to the hospital and the school. We had been told that we were relatively safe as long as we were lying below ground level during the bombardments. It was usually the children who heard the plane first. They could distinguish the sound of the Antonov from the sound of a cargo plane on its way to Juba. We had regular bomb alarms; the SPLA received a radio message when a bomber was in the air, but they did not know to which place it would fly. The alarm was rung and everybody was on the alert. Often we would sigh with relief when we learned a few hours later that the bomber had flown on to another place. We were safe for another day. Living in Torit was nerve-wracking but bearable.

But then on 5 June 1991 everything changed. Sister Josephine will never forget that day. She was walking in the corridor of the hospital when she heard the bombs falling. She started to run for the ditch, but a Sudanese doctor with a lot of war experience saw that it was too late for that. He grabbed Sister Josephine and threw her on the floor. Then the bombs started to explode all around them. 'Without that doctor I would have been dead', Josephine says now. When the explosions stopped and the doctor and sister got up, twenty-one people around them were dead and many more were wounded. Sister Lwanga and Sister Martha had reached the ditch: the children, as usual, had warned them in good time. The town mourned its dead, but the people in Torit were scared and the next day many of them started to leave the town for safer places in the hills. Nor did the sisters feel very safe, and they were responsible for the safety of the girls in their care. Maybe the time had come for them to leave.

In Imatong, forty kilometres from Torit, at the foot of the beautiful Imatong Mountains, they found a new home. The mountain provided some security against bombardment. There was a small clinic with hardly any medicines. There was a tiny school with no teachers. This seemed a suitable spot where the sisters could settle, or rather make a temporary abode. After all, missionaries should not settle down. There was no convent, and this was no time to build one. Nobody knew what turn the war would take or what the situation would be in a few months. That is how the idea of the tent convent was born. Four tents were bought for the sisters and a visitor. Two larger tents were erected alongside these: one would serve as the community and dining room and the other one would be the chapel. The new compound was ready in a few days. It was all very rudimentary but would do for the time being. Sister Josephine reopened the clinic and the small school soon became functional and respected. Many of the pupils had followed the sisters from Torit to Imatong. The sisters started their own gardens with the help of the bishop and the local people, and the bishop asked me to regard Imatong as my weekend parish. I would go there on Friday evening and return on Sunday evening or Monday morning. In that way the sisters would be able to attend the Eucharist at least a few times a week and on Sunday I would celebrate the Eucharist in the small church which the people had built. I felt a lot safer in Imatong than in Torit, where we still had the regular bomb alarms, and every six or seven weeks a bombing. I always looked forward to a weekend in Imatong.

But the administration of the SPLA also discovered that Imatong was a lot safer than Torit. Their decision to appropriate the school and the compound of the sisters as a training centre for the administration fell like another bombshell, this time not from the Khartoum government. The sisters wondered what the Spirit was telling them. They began to wonder whether this meant it was time to return to Uganda. The bishop reminded them that this kind of difficulty was precisely the reason why they had decided to build a convent of tents to remain flexible, as missionaries ought to be. The local people added their voice and begged the sisters not to leave Imatong. Was the Holy Spirit speaking through the bishop and the local people?

With the bishop, the sisters started to look around the Imatong area; they wanted to know where most of the people lived, which place was not too far from the road, where was there water close by for the children and themselves? The local chief joined them to offer advice. In the end they had sat down here under this tree, where we are sitting now, to rest and to discuss and evaluate what they had seen. The talkers were busy debating, but Josephine, not the talking type, was looking at the fig tree. It is enormous, perhaps more than a hundred years old. The branches hang on the ground and have taken root, so a circle of scions, still connected with the old tree, grows around the black rock on which we now sit. When the chief and the sisters finally asked Josephine where she thought they should go she had said, 'This place is as good as any and better than quite a few; the water is near and we are at the foot of the mountain which will be our shield against bombs.' She smiles when I ask her later whether that was the Holy Spirit speaking through her. The others had not directly thought of this place but as they looked at it a bit closer they all agreed. Only the chief had hesitated. This place was not just any place, and this tree was not just any tree. Here the Lutuko people prayed for rain; here they prayed for blessings for their people; here they brought their sacrifices. This was a holy place and not just anybody could come and live here. But when they went on talking it became clear that the sisters were not just anybody. Yes, the Lutuko people had prayed that they would have a clinic and they had hoped that they would have a school for their children. Maybe these sisters could be an answer to their prayers. The chief went to consult with the elders and Sister Martha knows that in the evening a goat was slaughtered and sacrificed under this fig tree to ask God's blessing over the decision to let the sisters live here.

A few days later, half of the local population was mobilized by the sisters and the bishop to build a new girls' school, a new clinic, and a sisters' compound. Next to the sisters' compound they built a small area with a hut where a visiting priest could stay. That is where I am sleeping tonight. Here, around this tree, the tents of the sisters were erected and a kitchen was built with an oven between two rocks. Latrines were dug, and the people built a fence from poles and grass. The bishop himself came for a week to Imatong to build together with the people. Everything was planned here on this rock without any building drawings being made, though this does not mean that everything was not carefully thought out; the people knew what had to be done as they proceeded.

The men brought bamboo sticks and poles. Women carried bundles of grass and water to make the mud for the walls of the classrooms. Men measured with pieces of string and put the first poles in the ground for the classrooms, whilst women stamped the mud for the walls. They mixed it with the soil of the anthills, knowing that it is ideal material for building walls and floors. After all, ants are master builders themselves. Indeed the work resembled the smooth co-operation of an ant colony, the people coming and going. It was not clear who was in charge, but it is all traditional work in which everybody knows their task; even children have their own job, for instance, looking after their smaller brothers and sisters while mother is busy in the mud pit.

And all this is done without money. There is hardly a money economy left in South Sudan. Even if you have money, there is little to buy with it. There are no shops left after the years of war. There are still a few weekly markets but with money you can buy only a few local vegetables; nobody will exchange a goat for money any more. We have here a barter economy in South Sudan. And here on this rock the bishop, the sisters and a few local leaders determined the exchange rate for the barter economy. A few cups of salt were paid for a bundle of grass, some washing soap for a few barrels of water, second-hand clothes for poles and bamboo. The people were not paid for their labour; that they provided free. It was they who had begged the sisters to stay here. But food was provided for everybody, which is the system when neighbours build a house together. Sister Martha had quite a few arguments with the bishop about the exchange rate. She reckoned out how long people in Uganda had to work to earn a pair of trousers, which people here could earn in just a day, by cutting bamboo and carrying it to the school site. Sister Lwanga would not allow it, saying, 'Don't criticize him, he is the best bishop.' But Martha answered, 'All right, he might be the best bishop, but I tell you, he is no businessman, he is far too generous.' The bishop laughed and said that the people were doing overtime, which had to be paid double. Within a few weeks everything had been built, even a dormitory for the girls.

Since the school was being built with the help of the local people it became clear that this would not be a boarding school exclusively for the girls from Torit. There the sisters had taught in English. Before coming to the Sudan they had learned some Arabic, but that was very much the language of the oppressor. Here they would have to use the local language, which the sisters still had to learn. So Sister Lwanga and Sister Martha started to teach some young people who knew English or Arabic, so they could teach the children in their own language. It was teacher-training on the job. An older woman teacher, who had been trained before the war, was found willing to start teaching here in the school of Imatong. The teachers do not get a salary, but every month they do receive soap, salt and food, as they don't have time to work in their own gardens. Twice a year they will receive some second-hand clothes. All these agreements have been contracted on this rock, under this tree, with all the old gods looking on, so no piece of paper was needed and nothing had to be signed. The school and the clinic run smoothly now.

Regularly, the people of Imatong bring some bananas for the sisters, or a woman brings a chicken for Sister Josephine, because a child, who was nearly dead, is running about again after treatment in Josephine's clinic. This morning somebody brought a few eggs for me. I asked, 'What have I done to deserve such a gift?' The simple answer was, 'You have come'.

Considering all these things, perhaps we missionaries *are* seen as good news by the local people. As we talk somewhat light-heartedly about what it means to be a missionary, here on this rock, it is clear that four missionaries seem to have four different visions about their missions. But it is also clear that quite a bit can be done before we have sorted out the theories behind our work. With a smile Sister Josephine adds once more, 'All that is needed is to remain open to the Spirit'.

A GOOD-FOR-NOTHING

*A human being doesn't survive because he
manages to kill all his enemies, but because he
succeeds in making more and more friends.*

Every week we come together in this small Christian
community. We meet in the house of one of the members
or, when that house is too small, under a tree. The small
Christian community is an attempt at supporting each
other in everyday life. The meetings are not strictly struc-
tured, but proceed somewhat informally, spontaneously;
after all, we must leave room for the Spirit. Usually part of
our meeting is a period of Bible sharing. Tonight there
are twenty of us sitting in the small courtyard of
Makokha's house. At the end of our last meeting Makokha
had said that we could meet in his home today and had
asked his neighbours to bring chairs, because he has only
two. It is a bit cramped but we all manage to find a place.

Together we read the Bible and we try to see what it has
to say about our lives here and now. We mostly read the
Gospel of the coming Sunday. In that way I also get some
suggestions for my homily. This evening we read the
Gospel of the weeds which grew among the grain,
(Matthew 13.24–30). The man sowed good seed in his
field, but his enemy came and sowed weeds among the
wheat. The weeds showed through when the heads of
grain began to form. The servants wanted to pull out the
weeds, but the master did not want this, afraid that they
might pull out the wheat with the weeds. He advised
them to wait till harvest time and only then to pull out
and burn the weeds while harvesting the wheat and

putting it in the barns. We had read the story but quite a few of the group are illiterate and they are inclined to think that they do not understand what is being read. So, after a silence the story is recounted by one of the participants, and we listen in a different way. Most members of our community who can read don't read very well, but many are good storytellers. Hearing the Gospel told freestyle, it becomes apparent to me that many of the Bible stories come from an oral tradition.

After this there is a silence and then gradually people start to share what the story means to them. Some share elaborately, others share just a short prayer. Again, we have not made too many rules about the procedure. People can share what they wish, and everyone listens with respect. One of the few rules is that there is no discussion of another's feelings and ideas: there is no right and there is no wrong in what somebody has heard in the reading or its retelling. People share freely, not shyly or self-consciously as we often do in other circumstances.

After some silence Makokha speaks.

'What I have heard today is beautiful, but', (and he looks sideways at me) 'it is different from what the missionaries have told us. I am that field and there is good and bad in me. But at times I do not know what is good and what is bad, but that has not to be my worry. The Lord knows, and the Lord will sort it all out in the end. I only have to grow.' Now he glances sideways once again, with a look in his face as if to say, 'I cannot help hearing what I hear'. Then adds once more, 'It is different from what we hear from the missionaries who tell us that we must get rid of all that is bad in us.'

At moments like this I am glad that we have the rule that we will not discuss what somebody shares. I don't have to answer Makokha who has a way of putting me on the spot, usually with a smile. We have become friends because I know his tribal language and that gives me some special standing with him. We often have talked together, especially when his son was in prison. At a party, after drinking a lot of local beer, the son and his cousin (in Africa, read 'brother'), got into a fight.

Makokha's son grabbed a knife. The fight ended with one person dead and Makokha's son in prison for manslaughter. He had been in prison for more than five years when I heard that he would be freed. His period in prison was shortened because of good behaviour. I accepted the job of going to collect him by car and Makokha had asked to come along with me. I knew that it was not an easy step for the man. On our way to the prison I tried to talk to him about it. What was it like to get your son out of prison? What did people say about it, and would he be welcome in the community again? Makokha's only answer was, 'My son is always my son'. In African society one is hardly ever rejected. People know that being human means making mistakes. Maybe Makokha has a point when he implies that we missionaries were often more concerned about eradicating what is evil than in cultivating what is good.

Often Makokha could smile about it when he was caught poaching. Yes, he knows that it is forbidden, but he can hardly afford to buy meat. For him, part of surviving is not getting caught. One way of doing that is by staying out of the limelight. Maybe he tries to live his own name. He has explained the name Makokha to me. In his tradition, when a child has died in the family, and a new one is born, the baby is taken away from the mother and placed somewhere outside, next to the road. Another person, usually a woman, is alerted and goes to find this baby and brings it back to the mother, shouting and telling everybody, 'Look, by the road I found some dirt, some rubbish' (perhaps we would say 'a good-for-nothing'). In that way the people hope to deceive the evil spirits, and prevent them from taking this new valuable life too. A good-for-nothing has a better chance of survival; evil spirits won't bother about him.

Makokha had learned to survive in this world, and he is by no means young any more. In some ways he is a wise old man, but at the same time he has still something of the naughty child in him. As I listen to him I hear them both. The wise old man, patient with all that is in him, and the naughty boy who with a smile puts the missionary on the spot.

I listen to Makokha and I think that he has a point. Perhaps we missionaries have been often too moralistic. It also might be that we have read the Bible only with our own eyes and have not listened to the Bible with African ears. Compared with listening to Makokha, it strikes me that it is easier for me to read one of the Church Fathers: I believe it was Saint Irenaeus who said, '*Gloria Dei est homo vivens*: God's glory is a human being fully alive'. In his own way Makokha is saying the same thing. It is true we often talk about a God of mercy, but for the Africans this is more a matter of course than it is for Europeans.

A few months later, when I am on leave in Holland, I talk with a friend of mine who is a Bible scholar. We talk about new approaches to reading Scripture and about new interpretations. He trots out the names of the current authors: the German scholar, Eugene Drewerman and some others. Yes, I have heard some of these names, but I have not taken the time to read them. I remember our Bible sharing in our Christian community and I think of Makokha implying that we missionaries did not preach the merciful God of the Bible. Often we seem to be more obsessed with not making mistakes than with doing good.

My friend is an academic and I am hesitant to introduce him to the thoughts of Makokha. I frame my approach with care: 'The Bible exegesis of many African theologians is often different from ours'. And I see he wants to know more. I tell him about the exegesis of Makokha, listening to the parable of the weeds in the wheat. I expect some criticism but I receive an enthusiastic response.

'You see,' my friend says, 'such explanations can only come from a continent which has not been heavily influenced by Calvinism as Europe has. We have all become Calvinistic in our thinking whatever denomination we are in Europe. European and American Christianity is Calvinistic whether we are willing to accept this or not. We are obsessed with the evil in our lives and we would not be able to understand the Bible in such a liberating way. Only an African theologian who is free from this Calvinistic thinking can listen in a different way. Who is this theologian and what has he published? I would like to read something of him.'

I tell him that this theologian has not written much, occasionally he goes to an adult literacy class, but he can hardly write his own name. My friend looks at me, 'Didn't you say that he was a theologian?' Yes, I did call Makokha a theologian, but then who isn't a theologian?

My friend smiles and he admits that he would have listened in a different way if I had said, 'An illiterate old man in the African bush gives this explanation of the passage'. However, this does not mean that he rejects the exegesis of Makokha, but it shows once more how prejudiced we are against oral cultures.

I am glad that the people were able to cheat the evil spirits at the time of his birth by calling him Makokha, just a little bit of dirt, a good-for-nothing. Maybe, with a friend like that, I will survive myself.

COUNT YOUR BLESSINGS

The ruin of a nation begins in the homes of its people.

Ashanti proverb

It is a strange experience, getting applause when you have just escaped death. We knew that the road between Kapoeta and Lokichokio was not always safe. People had been attacked there, and recently a driver had been shot. Occasionally, you could travel in a convoy with an armed escort of the SPLA, but this armed escort often attracted bullets rather than deflecting them. Now and again there was also a UN convoy: no armed escort, but not very secure either. We had discussed it, and we had been told that the local Taposa tribe had no quarrel with the church as such, and that it might be just as safe to travel by ourselves in the hope that we would not be attacked.

So that is what we had done, an American friend and I. Our Toyota Landcruiser was loaded with goods. Via Kenya and Uganda I was supposed to travel to Western Equatoria in Sudan. The robberies along this road were part of the government efforts to destabilize the area. We drove through the afternoon heat, in the hope that everybody was having a siesta. Then suddenly, in a bend of the track cut through the scrub-wood, he was standing there in the middle of the road. The man pointed an automatic gun at our faces. He remained motionless as I slowed down and stopped. He lowered his gun and came towards us. For a split second I considered putting my foot on the gas and trying to make a run for our lives. But then I heard the voices in the bushes around us and I felt that more guns were pointed at us. Not a word was said, but the man in front of us pointed with his gun that we should leave the car. I switched off the engine but I kept the key in my hands. With hands in the air, walking backwards, we moved away from the car. The other attackers came out of the bush and seven guns were directed at our faces. For a moment I thought that this was the end of my life. The men came towards us; they took my watch, and they demanded the beautiful Adidas sport shoes of my friend. I was lucky, my sandals were old and they did not look flashy. When they grabbed my cigarettes I thought; 'Just imagine that I had given up smoking in order not to get lung cancer and then they shoot me like this!' Then they started to unload our car and they called me as they could not open the back door. I was very helpful but at the same time very afraid. I carried the goods into the bush with them, and with the ten words of Arabic which I know, I tried to explain to them that I worked with the churches and that I was not involved in this war. We were talking to each other, and although we did not understand each other, the fact that we were trying to communicate with each other seemed to make the situation less dangerous. The car was no use to them, as ahead and behind us there were SPLA checkpoints. They let us keep the car. When I begged them for my passport, they could not understand that I could be interested in a small booklet like that and they gave it back to me. But the jerrycan of water they would not give back to me, as that was valuable to them.

I was trembling as I got into the car to drive on, I was afraid, and still angry and I was glad when I came to the SPLA checkpoint. Still shaken, I tell them what has happened to us. The young soldier looks quite impressed and calls one of his commanders. Again I tell our story and this man comes forward and slaps my back enthusiastically. 'You could have been shot dead, but you have survived. A few days ago they killed a driver, but they did not kill you. Congratulations!' The people who have gathered around us start to applaud. At first I don't know what to say, but then I have to smile; after all, they are right. I tell them that I was near to death, but they cele-

brate that I am still alive. My American friend lost his new
Adidas shoes, but they let me keep my old sandals and we
are amused about that too. It all becomes something of a
celebration; they lend me a small jerrycan of water and we
drive on.

This is not the first time I experience that the Sudanese
are more inclined to celebrate what they have, instead of
mourning what they have lost. Perhaps they would have
to mourn continually because they have lost so much. I
remember the time when we were bombed a few months
ago. My Sudanese friend, Nelson, and I jumped out of the
car and dived into the ditch along the road. We were lying
flat on our bellies when the first bomb exploded, too
close for comfort. I pressed myself deeper into the ditch
and I think I turned white. But Nelson burst out laughing
and shouted, 'We are still alive, they have missed us!'
Then we heard the second bomb falling, again the explo-
sion and I suppose that I turned whiter still, but my friend
was laughing, maybe also out of fear, and congratulated
me again: 'Mathew, we are going to make it, we will live!'
Trembling with fear, I said nothing. We saw the plane
turning around and it let loose two more bombs before it
disappeared. My friend jumped up and nearly danced for
joy that we were still alive. I got up, dazed and exhausted.
Another narrow escape. At moments like this I feel that I
want to leave Sudan, to be away from this war. A few days
later I am glad again that I am still here.

But being back in Bor was different. A few weeks earlier
I had been here to organize a workshop for the leaders of
the different churches. Going to Bor had been my first
visit to Dinka country. We had visited the cattle camps
along the road where the Dinka stay with their cattle for
part of the year in order to be close to the grazing
grounds. Bor is the diocesan centre of one of the
founders of the NSCC, Bishop Nathaniel Garang. He
wanted to form an inter-church committee to serve the
people better in times of real need. We held the workshop in Malek, one of the first mission stations of CMS,
the Church Missionary Society. Together we looked into
the needs of the people here and what contribution the
churches could make, and, as so often, the first request is

for relief. We know that some displaced people are on their way to Bor, and there is a real need for some emergency aid. But by the third day, people start talking about their priorities. There is hardly any talk now about relief food. They discuss a vaccination programme for their cattle, and a few hours later they have a draft plan worked out, covering a vaccination programme both for their cattle and their children. When I suggest that perhaps their children should come first, Margaret Aring, one of the women leaders stands up and says that cattle should be vaccinated first, because if the cattle die, the children will also die. Who am I to disagree with her? Cattle often come first with the Dinka people, in many ways it is their source of life. But after some time it is seen that the programmes could be combined, and the vets and nurses could travel together. The women leaders often were more realistic than the men. After four days we all had the feeling that slowly we were making progress.

Then we got a radio message from the UN advising me to leave this area and return to Torit, because they knew that there was going to be fighting here in Bor during the coming days. It is infuriating. They know that there is going to be fighting but they will not do anything about it. They only tell us, the whites, to leave the area as soon as possible. We discuss it, and many of the church leaders are well aware of the great tensions between different factions of the SPLA. They also think it is better that we leave. They themselves will see what has to be done, as they are used to war. They themselves can hardly leave with all their cattle; moreover they feel safer here close to the Nile. I decide that it is indeed better to leave, but deep inside I feel a bit of a deserter. Next morning we pack our Landcruiser. Unfortunately we can carry only a few sick people. It is strange to say goodbye to people, knowing that they are facing war in the coming days. What can one say? 'Good luck' does not seem to fit the situation. We stumble over our words, hoping that we will see each other again. They laugh about it and say, 'Who knows, maybe the troops on their way to Bor will never reach it'.

Unfortunately the information of the UN was accurate. Troops, mainly from the Nuer tribe, attacked Bor. For centuries there have been cattle raids and tribal fights, but now with automatic guns and other modern weapons it was a massacre, the Massacre of Bor of 1991. More than 3,000 people were killed including women and children who had not been quick enough to cross the Nile and hide in the papyrus as many of the men had done. Most of the cattle were killed or stolen.

About ten days after the massacre, we returned to Bor with a delegation of the NSCC. Many corpses were still lying about, people and cattle, though there had been an attempt at burning some of them. The place stank to high heaven. We drove again into Malek mission, where we were welcomed, but defeat filled the air. With no cattle, with no food, children were already dying. A supply of high-nutrient biscuits had arrived, but some children were too weak to eat them. The people had been promised some milk powder but that had not arrived yet. I looked around and I listened to some of the church leaders who told how it all happened, how some of them had been able to hide in the papyrus along the Nile, how others had been too late and had been slaughtered. I walked to the Nile and felt like vomiting, and I wanted to cry. This massacre was not perpetrated by Arabs against Africans, a war which somehow I had come to accept; these were southerners killing southerners, brothers killing brothers and sisters. It really made me sick and again I wanted to leave Sudan, and never return.

But then – I don't know where she came from – suddenly there was a woman standing next to me. Her face was somehow familiar, but only when she started talking about the workshop of a few weeks ago did I recognize Margaret Aring.

Margaret asked me to help her to organize a workshop with the leaders to get them to work together and see what could be done now, in this situation where everybody seemed defeated. Some leaders have died and now nobody knew who was in charge of whatever had to be done. Was this not the kind of situation that we should have been planning for a few weeks ago? I did not feel at all like talking to anybody, certainly not to arrange a workshop. I asked Margaret how she had survived. It was a gruesome story. She saw her husband being shot by the attackers when he tried to drive the cattle away into the shrubwood along the road. With her children she had run to the Nile, as many other people were running in that direction. A few boats were trying to take some women and children to the other side. But there were too few boats and there had not been enough time.

It was all too much of a scramble, Margaret tells me. She lost three of her children. She points at two young boys, not yet ten years old; these had been able to hide and they had survived. She had to make sure now that they would not die of hunger or of disease. It was not healthy that so many corpses were still lying around. The people had to be organized. For a while there is silence. Not so much that I don't know what to say, but because the moment asks for silence to remember the dead children. The story of Margaret Aring's family drives home the reality of the dispassionate reports about the Massacre of Bor. I knew her husband and I have also seen her children, who are now dead. I find it difficult to cope, now that numbers have become real people.

But then Margaret starts to talk again about calling people together to see how they can better organize the relief for the survivors. After the massacre, from 25,000 to 30,000 people are left behind in Bor, not dead, but many only half alive. All have lost family members, their cattle and their homes. Margaret has talked to some of the other women to see how together they could save their children and the families. This woman, who had lost so much, did not seem as defeated as I who had left Bor in good time to be safe in Torit. Somehow she has the energy to live now for her two surviving children and for the other survivors too. Compared to her, who was I to indulge in feeling defeated? I consider the situation hopeless but that is, perhaps, a luxury which only those can afford who can get away from this war. Margaret who wants to live on with her children does not give up hope.

With Margaret Aring we organized a meeting of some of the parents. The younger children especially were in danger of dying, and we ended the meeting with a plan for a feeding programme for children under five years old. They would be fed at the kindergarten. The UN was supplying biscuits and the Council of Churches would try to get some milk powder through.

The next day I drove back to Torit with some leaders of the churches who wanted to see their bishop. I was in a silent mood, angry about everything. When one of my friends, who always has a very positive attitude towards life, tried to engage me in conversation, I reacted callously: 'You always try to see things positively, you don't give up hope, but what can you say now that your own people are being killed by other southerners who a few months ago were still fighting with you for the liberation of the south? What have you to say to that?' He answered, 'I could say something, but it would only make you more angry.' We drove on in silence, disregarding that the road was rough and the day stifling. I was alone behind that steering wheel in a car full of people. Gradually the anger subsided and I glanced over at my friend who silently gazed out of the window. What were his thoughts? What had he wanted to say? He looked at me and said, 'You have studied philosophy, you have more than fifty years' life experience. Do you think that people have a greater capacity to do evil than to do good?' I had not expected this kind of question at this moment and I found it unfair, and I could see why he had been hesitant to ask this question an hour ago. When in the end I admitted that I did not think that a human being had a greater capacity to do evil than good, my friend said, 'What you have seen in Bor is an awful lot of evil.' Did he imply that also an awful lot of good could be done? And again I stayed silent.

JACK AND SORRO

*We speak in proverbs. Intelligent People
will understand us.*

Jack is a small-time father in the Netherlands. He has just
a field of asparagus and a patch of strawberries. The
asparagus and strawberries are not usually taken to the
auction, but Jack's wife sells them from the barn to the
tourists staying at the local campground. At first Jack had
been a little wary when the tourists came up to the barn.
But slowly he got used to them. Sometimes he even
hawked the strawberries round the holidaymakers'
cabins, and on rare occasions he even had a cup of coffee
or a beer with them. Many of the tourists were from
Germany. Jack is old enough to remember the Second
World War and he certainly was no fan of the Germans.
But he got to know them better and very gradually his
attitude towards them changed. The 'Jerries' became
'Germans' for Jack, and, later on, just regular people.
   Jack lives in a village not far from where I was born.
When I am in the Netherlands, on leave from Africa, I
usually go and visit him and his wife. He keeps me up to
date with the developments in the village. There were new
developments the last time I saw him. People from all over
the world, asylum seekers, had come to the Netherlands.
Gaining status as a refugee in the Netherlands is a process
that may take years, and there is no guarantee of obtaining
it. The people have to stay somewhere, and now the large
campground with its holiday bungalows has been turned
into a relief centre for those seeking asylum.

It had taken years for Jack to get used to the holiday-makers who overran his village in the summer. He never goes away on holiday himself; his vacations start when everyone has gone home and the village is his again. But now that the campground has become a relief centre, it is occupied all year round.

Jack is not pleased about it, and he is not the only one. I ask him if it is because the asylum seekers do not come to buy his asparagus and strawberries. No, Jack assures me, that is not the reason. 'The place is full of niggers, all kinds of brown scoundrels, fanatic Muslims and other strange people.' From the way Jack tells me it is quite clear that there is not much love lost between him and these people. There have been some robberies in the village. And he is not very happy that the people in the camp do not work. For Jack, work means working with your hands, farmer that he is.

Now I have known Jack for a long time, but in spite of his language this morning, it would not be right to call Jack a racist. I ask Jack whether he has met any of the asylum seekers. No, he has not. How could he? They don't even speak Dutch. The German tourists did not speak Dutch, but they at least understood Jack's dialect, which is related to German. He does not want to make life diffi-cult for anyone, and they do not all have to live the way he does, but he is at a loss with these people who have invaded his village.

'Now what about you?' Jacks wants to know, 'You have spent so many years with these blacks. How do you manage? Are they all like these foreigners here?' We had a good talk about this. The life of those seeking asylum is one of great uncertainty. They don't know whether they will be allowed to stay or not. They are like a ship in heavy seas, and they hold on to anything in order not to be sent back to their country of origin. Deep in his heart Jack is not against these people, but he does not want to be imprisoned in his own house behind locked doors, afraid that he might be robbed as others have been robbed. We talk further, but when I leave it is clear I have not fully convinced him. He remains afraid that they will break into his house. There may be thieves among those people, but they have not stolen his heart. 'We'll have to learn to live with it,' he says, and showing me to the door adds, 'I have no grudge against them, but I am not at ease with thieves around me. I worry my heart out. Believe me, many of those Africans are thieves, whatever you say.'

I return to Africa, to the Sudan this time, a country new to me. A new language again, and I wonder if I am still up to learning it. The gauntlet is thrown down when an old lady says to me, 'If you love us, you will be able to learn our language'. It is a slow business. Am I too old, or could it be that I do not love these people enough? I often feel they look at me with mistrust, and I think they do not understand me, but then it often happens that I don't understand them either. Just as it is for Jack, work for these people means working in the fields, and they never see me do that. I am a guest of these people, but in their eyes white people must seem a strange lot. Maybe I am in a similar situation to those Africans seeking asylum in the Netherlands.

This evening, as I sit with Sorro in the open near a log fire, I remember Jack and what we discussed. The moon is shining. We drink the sweet tea which Sorro's wife has poured for us. Sorro is older than I, and in Africa that means he is old enough to be wise. He knows the history of Sudan. Many of his ancestors were sold as slaves. He knows all about the European colonial oppression; he fought against it. But he also fought for freedom against the Arabs. Now he enjoys relative peace living at the edge of the forest with his wife and children.

Sorro is a member of the Anglican Church. He happened to be born in an area which had been allotted to Protestant missionaries in the colonial days. His wife was born in the next village, which was in the sphere of the Catholic Comboni missionaries. She was baptized a Catholic when she was in the primary school. When they married, the missionary told them that the Catholic church had very strict rules about the education of the children. But Sorro had his own rules. He had his sons baptized in the Protestant church and his daughters in the Catholic church. On Sundays they go to different churches, but every evening Sorro leads the prayers for his whole family at home. He is the help and mainstay of many. Missionaries and local priests spend the night in Sorro's home when passing through. Sorro and his wife are extremely hospitable. They have even built two extra rooms for all the guests who overnight there.

Back in Holland, Jack and I once discussed the great trouble there used to be between Protestants and Catholics. They even burnt each other's churches down. Now Sorro says how much he regrets that we missionaries brought a divided Christianity to Africa. The differences between the Catholics and Protestants have very little to do with African realities. I agree with him. He tells me about the tension there often was, and still is, between whites and blacks, between Arabs and the blacks, and between the African tribes.

We discuss how people who have fought each other for so long will be able to work together again, when there will be peace again in Sudan. To him, peace is more than the absence of war. As we sit here this evening, I feel convinced that this man is really at peace, in spite of the war all around him.

Here, in the middle of Africa, I remember Jack's question, 'How do you manage, working with people who are so different?' Jack had grave doubts with his, 'I worry my heart out.' Sorro's stories make it obvious that co-operation and mutual understanding is not a story of unqualified success in Sudan either.

With the moon looking down on us I put Jack's question, which is also mine, to Sorro. How can there be more understanding between peoples? How can we get to know each other's worlds and show greater respect for each other's views? Sorro does not read books, and in fact I am expecting one of those long stories about Africa he often tells. But his reply is no long argument. Sorro's wisdom does not come from books; he knows the sayings and proverbs of his tribe, and there is much wisdom in these sayings: *proverbs are the daughters of wisdom*. He has understood my question all right; in some ways he lives the answer. Sorro gets along with everybody; he is one who truly loves people. As he throws some more wood into the fire, the flames light up his face. Looking at me, he says, 'You want to look through my eyes? Give me your heart and I shall give you my eyes.'

I ponder these words of Sorro and know deep in my heart that Jack is not the only one who says or thinks, 'I worry my heart out'. I do not give my heart away that easily. Maybe it is true that some of these Africans are thieves; they may steal your heart.

A GOD-ORDAINED LAYMAN

A kind lie is better than a violent truth.
Maasai proverb

It is not the first time we find ourselves together in a difficult spot. For years Ongwech and I have been conducting workshops together: with others we search for ways for further growth. Calling it consciousness-raising is perhaps a bit over the top. When people of goodwill become aware of why things go wrong between them, they might agree to embark on a new way; then some change may well come about. That is the general idea of these workshops. But it is a slow process, for new ways are not easy to find or follow. There are always those who profit from the existing order or disorder, and want to keep things as they are. Then too, those people who want to take a new path may feel uncertain, rightly so, because success is not guaranteed. It all comes down to human effort.

It is no different in the Church. The participants in this workshop are a mixed bag: priests and laity, white and black, religious of various origins, tired and frustrated people, and others full of enthusiasm who want to get cracking. Tonight Ongwech conducted the last session and made a fine job of it. Many matters that had been bottled up for years were voiced. The ingratitude for their dedication felt by missionaries was set off against the frustration of Africans who, even in their own country, had not been consulted by the western priests and religious before they set to work. The paternalism of the missionary was brought up, the alienation of the African priest from his own culture, the lay people who just go their own way, and African and European nuns who though living in one community are strangers to each other: all these matters were raised. And all this within this Catholic Church of ours, which we all feel so involved in and committed to. When all is said and done, that is why we are gathered here in this workshop. After the session was over, the discussion continued outside. The atmosphere was charged and painful.

Now Ongwech and I are talking about tomorrow morning's session. Ongwech is relaxed, lying on his bed in our shared room. I sit on the side of mine, uneasy. I don't thrive in crisis situations, and at times it seems as if Ongwech is trying to provoke them. He often points out to me that every crisis creates new opportunities. Now he is suggesting that I conduct the next session. Some of the priests and religious feel threatened after the last one, and Ongwech thinks they will more readily accept the leadership of a priest than that of a layman. 'To them I'm "only" a layman', he says with a smile.

How are we to get this group closer together again? I ask myself. I put that question to Ongwech too. 'Not in the Dutch way', he responds with a smile. I can hardly change my national heritage on the spot, and act as if I am African. 'What's wrong with our way?' I ask. He turns over on his bed. Ongwech knows our kind; he has worked together with many Dutchmen, he visited our country, had Dutch teachers in school. 'You see,' he says, 'you people think that honesty is the greatest virtue. One must always tell the truth. But you use truth as a weapon, and if someone takes offence you shrug your shoulders and say, "Well, that's the truth, isn't it?" As if that justifies hitting someone over the head with it.' He says this with a wry grin on his face, which softens this 'hard' truth a little.

'But surely, honesty is a virtue', I object.

'Oh, without a doubt, but not the greatest. Love is the greatest, according to the Bible', answers Ongwech. I ask if he is suggesting I should let all truth go by the board. At times I get the impression truth is not always taken seriously in Africa. Ongwech reflects on this, then answers, 'You must tell the truth, but not every truth must be told.

And if you have to tell the truth, a little subtlety is better than a lot of force.'

This is another of those truths Ongwech has a knack of coming up with. When the two of us travel together by car, or when we share a room, he likes contrasting his thoughts with mine. Ongwech is a thinker, and he often thinks aloud. Long ago he was a devout student, scoring high marks at the junior seminary. One of his Dutch professors in the major seminary even thought he might make a good bishop later on. But the bishop never ordained Ongwech. As a philosophy student he was inclined to ask very awkward questions. He wondered if praying was a more spiritual occupation than tilling the soil or sleeping with a woman. Ongwech will not be the only African to wonder about this, but he is probably one of the few to ask his professor of philosophy. The professor had no clear-cut answer, for he did not till the soil, nor did he sleep with women. When one day there was a strike at the seminary and Ongwech was the students' spokesman, he was marked as a troublemaker and the white bishop decided that Ongwech had no vocation.

It was one of these crises which creates new opportunities, if one is open to them. Ongwech left the seminary but really had no doubts about his vocation: one way or another he wanted to be a priest. He was still quite conscious of his roots and felt compassion for his country and its exploited people. He devoted his life to the consciousness-raising of the community. He fights for liberation from all that makes people less human. He does not see his own culture as something static, as something that cannot change, but at the same time he is critical of influences from the West. When we talk about inculturation, Ongwech will point out that foreign missionaries are part of a deculturation process. He knows the missionaries, has no hostile feelings against them, but he does point out regularly that we too have our limitations. He often does this in a devious way, by asking apparently quite innocent questions.

Once, at a funeral, a young missionary had great trouble saying the prayers in the tribal language. The missionary had to struggle to pronounce the words correctly, and in any case the prayers of the funeral ritual did not seem to fit the African context. After he was finished with his stumbling, the catechist and the elders prayed with great fervour. They did not need a book; their hearts were full of prayers. The missionary was sidelined, in spite of his cassock and stole. Ongwech asked me without guile, 'Is the catechist less a priest for these people than the ordained missionary?' We talked about it, and we came to the conclusion that there is a lot of priesthood in Africa and probably elsewhere in the world which is overlooked by the Church. And lightheartedly we wondered whether God perhaps secretly ordains men and women who are overlooked by the bishops. Luckily we cannot control God's Spirit.

Ongwech can be very captivating when speaking about the Spirit of God at work in every human being if only we let him. He is a deeply religious man, but he thinks the foreign missionary tries to control even that Spirit. During one of our conversations about 'unfathomable' Africans and 'unfathomable' Europeans, he again came up with one of his simple and slyly stupid questions: 'Wherever did you get the idea of writing prayer books or books on how people must love one another? Is it possible to lay down hard and fast rules for the human heart?' I myself find these books helpful, but in formulating a response, I discover that his question is more incisive than simple and stupid. We do indeed often kill the creativity of the human heart. Ongwech's reflections and prayers during our services often fit in with the reality of the world around us, and they come from deep inside him, not from a book. I have no answer for many of his simple questions but many of them are worth having, even without answers.

So, Ongwech has just told me that the 'shoot-from-the-hip' approach is not the right one for tomorrow morning. I tell him that I can hardly do as if I am an African, and that at times I find their endlessly beating about the bush almost corrupt. Ongwech smiles when I say my piece. It even gets him up from the bed, and he begins to search in his well-thumbed Bible. He always has that small Bible with him; he has undefined texts that have a special meaning for him. Does not everyone pick and choose from it? He glances through the book and says: 'There are some words of Christ you missionaries do not preach or talk about, perhaps because you think Christ is also a bit corrupt. Perhaps he was more of an African than a Dutchman.' Then, sitting in his shorts on the bed, he reads, 'Remember, I am sending you out to be like sheep among wolves; you must be cunning then, as serpents, and yet as gentle as doves'. (Matthew 10.16). He looks at me with those twinkling eyes. I show a faint smile: yes, at times, we think that cunning is corrupt and yes, we Dutch are not particularly gentle characters. I do recognize some of that text in the African life. Ongwech has got some of it. I have always put it down to 'the African in him'. For himself he says that it is also the Christian in him.

'But now about tomorrow morning. What will be the best way for me to lead the group in dealing with all the tensions which surfaced at the last session? How should I tackle it?' I want to map out a clear line of action. 'Come on, Ongwech, let's hear your suggestion.'

'Must your line of action be a straight one?' he wants to know. He says he does not know a clear way; some participants will be obstacles, others will function as bridges. 'Just imagine,' Ongwech continues, 'We are in a jungle, the two of us and we want to get out of that jungle. I have the impression that you want a map or even want to draw one yourself. Are you tense because you don't know the way?' Ongwech does not want to map out the way. He knows that people who walk together in the forest create a path as they are walking. He proposes that we conduct the session together, without a clearly-mapped road. 'As we go along, we will find a way.' Ongwech will be my guide tomorrow and that gives me the courage to set off again with the group.

As usual with Ongwech and me, it is late when we switch off the light and try to sleep. It does not take long for him to drop off. I am grateful that he is here with me. He is often my guide, in some ways my spiritual director. I remember our conversation about the funeral. I wonder if Ongwech was secretly ordained by God, when his bishop decided he had no vocation. For me he is a good shepherd, cunning and gentle.

SOCIAL SERVICES OR
ECONOMIC SERVICES?

He who eats alone, will die alone.
Kikuyu proverb

Philip proudly shows me his diploma. A recommendation
of his parish priest helped him a few years ago to gain
admission to the teachers' training college. Before he was
qualified he had been teaching in some of our schools for
a few years. He was zealous. Not only the priest, but also
the education board thought he deserved that recommendation. He did well in the college, and he is a qualified
teacher now. He looks smart in his trousers of the latest
fashion, bright shirt and modern sports shoes. He is one
of the new generation of teachers shortly to be posted to
one of our schools.

That is what he is coming to see me about. You see, he
has a girlfriend. She has not finished her studies yet, but
they want to get married before long. Weddings are
expensive, her parents are rather traditional and Philip
thinks he will not be able to escape the dowry. He also
wants to build a house with a roof of corrugated iron.
Everything is expensive and he has had no chance to save
any money. At the end of the month everyone in the
whole family expects a little: grandma needs a blanket, his
brother needs a school uniform, a cousin looking for
work asks for part of the bus fare to town, and on and on.
It just never stops.

Philip has been thinking hard about this. He knows I
usually attend the meetings of the education board. In the
Catholic-sponsored school I even have a say about which

teachers are appointed there. Could I please put in a word for him? If he is posted in a school far away from his family, he thinks he may be able to start a life of his own. His salary is meant to keep one family, but you cannot provide for half a tribe, although some seem to expect so. I understand Philip's argument. Young people should be given a chance, and I promise to talk things over with the education board. He feels relieved when he goes home.

One of the agenda items for the education board meeting is the appointments for the coming scholastic year. The members have been elected by the parish council, the teachers, and some have been suggested (not to say forced upon them) by the parish priest. Alexis, an old teacher, chairs the meeting. In making the decisions, an individual's circumstances are taken into account: a lady teacher with small children is posted close to home; one teacher, given to drink, is posted under a headmaster who can exercise some authority over him. Alexis is already old. They say his hair has gone grey but that he dyes it black with charcoal. His suit and tie are old too. His suit is shiny from all the washing and ironing, but he attends every meeting neatly dressed, and his patched-up shoes are well polished. He chairs the meeting with an air of wisdom. He is one of his tribe's elders, one of the first teachers in this area. Without him there would be many a clash in the parish council between the parish priest and the members of the board. He always agrees with the priests and yet knows how to find a way of getting the proposals of the members accepted.

When the postings of the new teachers are under discussion I put in my word for Philip. Alexis says he can understand the problem and suggests he himself will have a word with Philip. A little later someone suggests that Philip would fit in very well in a school which happens to be quite near his home, quite contrary to what Philip had asked for. They need a teacher there who could introduce the new method of teaching English. Alexis nods his approval and says Philip will certainly understand after Alexis has discussed it with him. I have my doubts, but because Alexis proposes that he himself should talk it over with Philip, I leave it at that. If Philip does not agree

I am sure he will come and tell me. But I do feel like an outsider at this meeting, the only one who does not know what is really going on. I am not so certain that Philip is really needed in that school so near his home.

After the meeting, Alexis tarries a bit, leaning on his much-welded bike. After years of service as a teacher he has not gathered much wealth. He still does not own one of those houses with a roof of corrugated iron, yet he is a respected man, both in civil and in ecclesiastical circles. When I invite him for a cup of tea, he puts his bike back against the wall. Sitting on the veranda together I ask him why Philip's request has not been granted. The question does not surprise him; maybe he tarried a bit just to answer that question.

He starts by explaining how much good the missionaries have done. He mentions the schools, the many parishes. Eighty per cent of his tribe is Christian. Alexis is grateful for that. He plays an active role in the church. His people have received so many good things and Alexis says: 'He who has received much, should give much'. But not everything that is good for the white man, is necessarily good for Africa. 'We must be good Africans, if we want to be good Christians', he says. Alexis speaks about honouring one's father and mother, who to an African means more than the people who brought you into the world. Nobody is an island in Africa: without family, without your friends, you are nobody.

Now take Philip, for instance. Alexis knows that family. The young teacher started his schooling late because his parents could not pay the fees. Then one of his uncles, who had a job, gave the first fees. Many in the family helped Philip to continue his studies. Even cows reserved for the dowry of Philip's sister-in-law were sold. Philip has become a teacher with the support of the entire clan. Without the help of many he would be still herding cattle. And now that he is able to make his first contribution to his family, he walks out on them; he wants to sever the umbilical cord which has nourished him for so long. 'As Christians we should not condone that.' Does Philip not know that you marry not only a woman but all her relatives as well, that you marry a family? Will he, once he is

married, not need the help of his family and the clan? Oh,
it is the influence of the mission that uproots the young
people. A man must be well-rooted in his tribe, in his
clan, in his family. As a man on his own he will be lost,
even if he has all the money in the world.
Of course, Alexis is not altogether wrong. But, I
explain, times are changing. On our side of the world
things were once different too. But you cannot stop
progress. I explain to him the ins and outs of society in
Europe: free education, all the social services. Philip, with
his taxed salary, pays for social services too, does he not?
In a few years Alexis will be drawing a pension, admittedly
not a large one, but it is a beginning. Granted, social
services here are rather poor, but a man like Alexis should
be fighting to improve them, I suggest, instead of continuously hammering on the tradition of his tribe.
Alexis does not openly disagree with me. He has more
questions about these European social services. I explain
them all, including the old age pension. 'You mean you
say you don't support even your own mother?' he asks
incredulously.
'Of course I do, Alexis, we pay taxes to the government
and the government gives my mother her old age
pension.' The old teacher tries to grasp whether he has
understood me correctly. Do I say that I do not support
my mother, but that I pay money to the government to
support my mother? Alexis does not quite see how we can
call that a 'social' service. In his view this is 'antisocial', or
at least 'a-social'. He freely admits that Europe's economic
structure is better than Sudan's, but the social services in
his tribe are better, he thinks, and with them come
commensurate social obligations. Alexis has never tried to
avoid them; he has always shared whatever he had in
riches, influence and wisdom. It has not made him rich, at
least not what one may call economically well off. Still, he
feels wealthy. He has been of service to his clan, and he
knows they will never leave him in the lurch. After talking
to Alexis, I can accept the proposed posting for Philip,
and trust that he will talk Philip around to accepting it.
It has been years since I had this conversation with
Alexis. At that time I still thought that western culture was

transcendent in many ways. Alexis just could not grasp why we called economic services, those that deal essentially with money, 'social' services. I had thought that he was trying to have me on. But now, many years later, I begin to see his point: in our western society we may have good economic services but we do not distinguish them from social services, whereas Africa still has true social services.

THE SUIT OF ARMOUR

Pain is a gift: if caused by warriors
look upon them as your fathers.

Maasai saying

Although I have spent many years in Africa, it does not mean that I have become an African. I look at things with European eyes and Africans look at the West with African eyes, and what they see is often very strange. Africans have many questions about European ways and it is not always easy to answer them. I once attempted to explain to a group of Africans a photograph of the *Elfstedentocht*, a long-distance skating race in Friesland, in the Netherlands. For people who have no idea of winter, who do not know what ice or snow is, and what 'hard, slippery water' is, it is absolutely beyond them.

This morning, however, I thought I had an easy one. Two men were glancing through the magazines lying on my table. They cannot read and because of that they are all the more interested in the pictures. As I pass through the room, the two of them are studying the picture of a knight in a suit of armour: helmet, breastplate and everything that goes with it. It is in an article about the life of knights in the Middle Ages. One of the men wants to know: 'Well, what's this? Isn't this man strangely dressed, even for a European?' I think: I can handle this one and need not think long about an answer.

'Look, this is how in the olden days our warriors used to fight. That's an iron suit, the warrior is covered from head to toe, and cannot possibly be wounded by arrows or spears. That small screen in front can be lowered and then even his eyes are shielded. But a particularly brave warrior wouldn't use it: he would fight the enemy with the visor open.' I thought I had done very well in explaining this. These men had been warriors themselves, the scars on their bodies attest to it, and I thought they would consider such a suit of armour quite a useful invention. And I walk out and leave them to it.

When I return, the men are sitting there chuckling as if one had just told a dirty joke. Had I said something stupid again? I ask them what the joke is. Aupai, the elder one, who is reputed to have been a brave warrior and wrestler, says, 'So that's how you people fought, eh? And what about the women?'

'Are women warriors?' I ask. 'The women didn't fight, of course, but they often looked on at the duels.' No, they understand that women did not join in the wars, 'But did the warrior who fought in such a suit of armour still succeed in getting a wife?'

'Why would he not get a wife?' I don't quite get what these men are talking about, and Aupai tries to set me straight.

We have been to circumcision ceremonies together. The young lads are circumcised with the whole community looking on. It is a very painful operation and the pranks the circumcisor pulls with his knife are not what one might call comforting. However, the young men do not flinch, do not even bat an eyelid, while the circumcisor does his job. During the weeks of preparation they have been trained to face up to pain. The community standing around admired them and accepts them as full members of their society. Pain is almost celebrated here. The entire community, so to speak, embraces the boy undergoing the pain. The pain is not camouflaged and no one says soothingly: 'It only takes a second', or 'It doesn't really hurt', as a European might be inclined to say. The community will sooner say: 'Boy, this will hurt, but you can stand it, because you are one of us, we're with you.' Such brave men are ready for responsibility; wives can be entrusted to them. An uncircumcised man will not get a wife.

'Why are you whites so afraid of pain?' Aupai wants to

know. And I have no clear answer. First, I want to say that this is not true. But so much in our society is indeed aimed more at avoiding pain than at being happy. We have got used to insuring ourselves against anything that may be painful or uncomfortable: I think of the Disability Act, Unemployment Benefits, Compulsory Health Insurance, even the Burial Insurance. And if some pain does come our way at times, we have ways and means to kill it. It's not that I disapprove of this, but these old Africans seem to look at it quite differently.

'Suffering and pain aren't good things', I say bluntly.

'No, they are not, but you should not be afraid of them, don't avoid them; Jesus did not run away from pain and suffering.' I very much feel like saying: 'Tell me another!' Shutting out pain means shutting out all happiness. These men laugh at a life that concentrates on avoiding pain. They remind me of the Arab saying, *Only sunshine makes a desert.*

Abstract arguments are not particularly in Aupai's line. But he knows that I have sometimes watched his people's wrestling matches. The fighters are naked. This sport is a mixture of wrestling and boxing. Aupai has fought many a bout. Like many Africans he is proud of the scars. You take quite a beating, but the entire village is watching and encourages and applauds you. The winner is carried around on their shoulders, he is slapped on the back, and the women and girls vie to touch him.

That's why Aupai and his friend had such a good laugh at that silly knight in his suit of armour. He may have protected himself very well against all pain, but how is a woman to embrace him? Of course, Aupai is right; if we can no longer be hurt, it is impossible for us to be embraced or loved. In my explanation of the picture I had pointed out that the open visor was a sign of courage; these men, however, dare me to remove my entire suit of armour. That will take some courage.

I have no wish to re-open the argument with Aupai, but for myself I am glad that those brave African warriors often carry a small shield. There is nothing wrong in seeking a little protection. Not a full suit of armour, but a small shield will do.

PEACE AMBASSADORS
WITHOUT PORTFOLIOS

*The worm does not force its way in: it gently
persuades the soil. That's the worm's way of
being allowed into the soil.*

Azande proverb

We are participating in a workshop set up by an aid organization to focus attention on the forgotten civil war in
Sudan. The government in Khartoum has come in for
heavy criticism from all sides, but an Italian missionary in
the group forcefully demurs, giving his experiences of his
regular flights into southern Sudan in support of fellow
missionaries. He lashes out against the southern liberation movement, the SPLA, alleging that there is ample
evidence of their frequent infringement of human rights.
An embarrassed silence follows his outburst. He has not
been making this up. The facts are there in all their stark
reality.

A local commander of the SPLA had raided the mission
post early one morning. He had arrested two sisters, an
American missionary and a Sudanese priest. The whole
compound was searched and looted and the missionaries
were accused of being government agents. They were
held prisoner for a number of days and not treated very
gently. The Italian missionary had been alerted in Nairobi,
and with a colleague had flown to plead with the
commander for the release of the prisoners. He had been
received with ill grace and was lucky not to have been
taken prisoner himself. Back in Nairobi he had contacted
the international media and the Council of Churches to
put pressure on the SPLA. The international media are a
powerful weapon. John Garang, the leader of the SPLA,

had to take notice and promised to look into the affair. Soon after this, the missionaries were indeed set free, but the property stolen in the raid was not returned. Dr Garang had also promised an apology, but none came, certainly not in writing. Even though the peace initiative had been a partial success, the missionaries had not gained all they wanted. The SPLA had not been impressed by their approach. Is that why now the SPLA is put in the dock here? The deceptively calm demeanour of the Italian missionary belies his underlying feelings of deep anger and frustration. All Sudanese eyes are intently fixed on the floor. I wonder what they are thinking. They have so many proverbs which fit this situation. Maybe they think 'Don't throw mud in the well of your host', or 'If someone beats your goat, you don't go and kill his bull'.

This certainly is not the first clash between the SPLA and representatives of the churches. Undoubtedly, none of the southern Sudanese present would approve of the line of action taken by the SPLA commander, yet they remain silent. Bishop Paride Taban looks like the meaning of his name, tired, exhausted. This usually vigorous man is immensely weary as he listens to this story. A few hours ago, when we were alone, he had told me his version of the story which had just been told here. 'The SPLA make grave mistakes', he had said, 'but we too make mistakes. Was it the task of expatriate missionaries to denounce the forced recruitment of children into the ranks of the SPLA, or should that have been left to the children's parents? Should foreign church leaders put pressure on the freedom fighters, or had the Sudanese bishops failed in their responsibilities?' He is by no means less critical of the freedom fighters than the Italian missionary but his approach is strikingly different. I know that he pulls no punches in private encounters with the SPLA leadership, and they respect him for it. But he is very aware that everyone stands to lose if all fight to win. During that painful silence, I was reminded of a similar incident in southern Sudan that had involved me and Bishop Paride.

At the time we were in Nairobi, Kenya, when the SPLA leader, Dr Garang, spread the news that one of his rivals, William Nyoun, had abducted a priest from the diocese of

Bishop Paride some weeks previously. This, it was alleged, was a clear sign that William Nyoun was against the churches and in the pocket of the Khartoum government whose hostility towards Christians was common knowledge. As Paride tells me the details I am inclined to believe the rumours. When I ask the bishop what he thinks, he replies that the churches should not take sides in the rivalries within the SPLA. The story could be fabrication, but Paride also knows his priests. He knows that Father Joseph Okello, the priest in question, is not exactly a model diplomat. He may well have got on the wrong side of Commander Nyoun with some 'loose-cannon' comment or other.

My instinct is immediately to alert the media to exert pressure on the parties involved, but the bishop insists that the story be verified first. Fortunately Lafon, the mission station where the alleged abduction took place, is connected to the outside world by radio. Bishop Taban raises the station and diplomatically inquires whether he may speak with Joseph Okello. He has to be careful because any talk of military matters over private wavebands is banned. Okello has gone on safari, he is told, and no one knows when he will be back. Would it be possible to talk to Commander Nyoun? He too, is out of the station and no one knows when he will return. The bishop realizes that he is being stonewalled. Whatever has happened cannot be discussed over the air.

Bishop Taban reflects for a while and asks me if there are any friends of Sudan of some political status, at present in Nairobi, who might be prepared to fly to Lafon? I know that there are plenty. Monsignor Kaut, who represents the German aid organization *Missio* has already indicated that he wishes to visit southern Sudan. The fact that he knows Joseph Okello is a bonus. Furthermore, there is a delegation of the organization, Norwegian Church Aid, headed by a bishop. They support several projects in the neighbourhood of Lafon. William Nyoun can hardly ignore them since the aid is vital for people in the region. A Belgian Member of Parliament and some friends are also prepared to come along. 'Quite an impressive delegation with considerable clout', I tell

Bishop Paride with glee. He hardly hears my remark, and
appears deep in thought about what lies ahead, though
he is hardly perturbed. He seems to know exactly how to
handle this kind of crisis.
It is Friday. He tells me to charter a small aircraft for
Monday and to invite the guests to come along. The
Norwegian contingent will charter a plane for themselves,
and they stress that they can exert pressure through
contacts in Europe. Bishop Paride asks them to limit
themselves to 'being guests and looking important'. Of
course, being a guest does not combine well with throw-
ing your weight about. He asks me to accompany him as
representative of the New Sudan Council of Churches,
and to organize the flight for the guests. A few hours later
he radios Lafon: 'On Monday morning I will be coming to
Lafon with friends of Commander William Nyoun and
Father Okello. These friends are from Germany, Norway,
Belgium and the Netherlands. They would like to meet
Joseph Okello and William Nyoun to discuss various
projects and programmes with them.'
On Saturday morning he sets off northwards for Sudan.
We agree to pick him up in Nimule on our way to Lafon.
On Sunday morning there are rumours that Joseph Okello
has been shot dead whilst attempting to flee. This is soon
followed by a radio message from Bishop Paride telling us
to follow our plan as agreed earlier. Grave doubts about
the wisdom of this course begin to trouble the 'Important
Guests'. How far can one trust the likes of William Nyoun?
If he has ordered the killing of Joseph Okello, who will
guarantee the safety of our delegation? I too have my
doubts, but I trust the wisdom and experience of Bishop
Taban. *Don't try to show a gorilla the way in the forest*,
they say in Africa.
We are all tense when we fly to Nimule to pick up
Bishop Taban. Some of the party discuss ways of exerting
pressure on William Nyoun. The money behind our delegation must provide considerable leverage. Many of us on
the plane want to help actively, make a contribution, do
something. It is not easy to be mere onlookers in a drama
played before our eyes. The passive role we have been
assigned seems insignificant. Bishop Taban wants us to

'be impressive', whilst we prefer to exert power. During our short stopover in Nimule, Bishop Paride tells us that he has heard from well-informed sources that Joseph indeed has been arrested, but is still alive. 'Good news', he says. The Cessna Caravan takes off again and twenty minutes later we land on the bumpy airstrip between the rocky outcrops of Lafon.

A heavily-armed military detachment in brand-new uniforms is waiting for us. We observe them somewhat warily from the relative safety of our window seats. A few indulge in some macho military posturing. Bishop Paride is the first to leave the plane, and all the soldiers come smartly to attention. He ignores the military display and walks up to Commander William Nyoun. They hug as old friends after a long separation. Then he shakes hands with the soldiers, further defusing the tension. The Important Guests are introduced one by one, and the soldiers applaud. Commander Nyoun recognizes me from the time when we both lived in Torit, a few years ago. He often came to see me then to ask for pens and paper for his soldiers. He has had little formal schooling himself, but he has a reputation for being a formidable fighter. I too receive a friend's welcome.

Then we all sit down in the shade of a few large trees. The Important Guests are given chairs whilst the soldiers stand in a circle around them and the villagers watch the proceedings from a safe distance. We talk about the war, which everyone seems to condemn, about the lack of emergency aid, healthcare and a host of other issues, but not a word is uttered about Joseph Okello. A soldier, to whom I once gave a few copybooks when we were in Torit together, has let me know that Father Joseph is somewhere in Lafon. Rumour has it that he was arrested when he told his parishioners that they should not co-operate with William Nyoun because he is a Khartoum government stooge.

At some point during the discussions, the Norwegian bishop explains to William that rumours circulate in Norway that his faction of the SPLA actively co-operates with the Khartoum government. 'What is your reaction to these rumours?' I feel a surge of unease because I know

that it is remarks of this kind that got Joseph Okello into
trouble in the first place. But William is unruffled. A guest
is allowed to speak his mind. He answers very calmly:
'You see, I am a Nuer. We are cattle herders but we also
fish for a living. When you want to catch fish you have to
go to the river. My opponent, Dr Garang, has blocked the
way to the rivers called Uganda and Kenya. The only rivers
I can reach are Juba, Torit and Kapoeta. That is where I go
fishing and from time to time I catch something.'
   I listen in amazement at what William has to say. Juba,
Torit and Kapoeta are towns firmly in the hands of the
Khartoum government. A few guests cast a questioning
glance in the direction of Bishop Taban. Is this a brazen
admission of co-operation with the Khartoum government, seen by everyone here as the evil oppressor? The
bishop does not react. Surely he must realize that those
new uniforms and guns originate from government stores
in Juba and Torit, and are part of the catch William was
referring to. Instead of making a direct comment he asks
William if he knows the story of the father and the son?
   The bishop is a seasoned raconteur. Everyone, Sudanese
and visitors alike, prick up their ears.
   'There was a man who lived in the bush with his son.
He had a small chunk of antelope meat and made ready to
prepare it for himself and his son, but the fire had died.
So he sent his son to look for fire. The son set off and
soon caught sight of a reddish glimmer in the under-
growth. In his childish innocence, he thought it was fire
and ran to get it. Who could describe his consternation
when suddenly he found himself staring into the gaping
jaws of a mighty lion? The reddish glow he had seen was
nothing other than the lion's gums! With great presence
of mind he addressed the lion, saying: "Uncle lion, I have
been sent by my father. He has caught an antelope and
invites you for a meal." The lion felt greatly honoured at
being respectfully called Uncle, and after all, an antelope
was a lot more appetizing than this skinny little fellow.'
The bishop pauses to make sure he holds our attention,
and drives home the point: 'Thus the son saved his own
life by guiding the lion to his father's house. You can
commend him for his cunning. For the moment he is out

of danger. But the lion will make short shrift of the left-over chunk of antelope. It won't last. And who do you think will be next on the lion's menu?'

All the while William has been listening attentively and now he laughs somewhat sheepishly. The meaning is not lost on him. He does not deny that he co-operates with the government. He must be aware that it is a risky alliance. Bishop Paride goes on explaining that the children of the same family do not always think the same, that there are differences of opinion in every family and that there may be fierce rows. Such disputes concern the whole family and we are here together as one family, with even some distant uncles from far away. And we have talked. But there are also matters that need to be discussed in the privacy of the small family circle. The uncles do not need to be present then. He proposes that I show those uncles how Lafon has been devastated by this never-ending conflict.

We leave Paride and William behind in a tent. I know that now they will no longer speak in parables or fables. There will be some very straight talking. Whilst I show the visitors the terrible destruction wreaked on Lafon, the commander and the bishop talk with one another. We walk around in the village. Many people have been killed here; any survivors fled. After many months, they are back now and have started rebuilding their huts in the shadow of those enormous rocks. Strictly speaking, the people here want nothing to do with the SPLA or with the government. They just want to be left in peace to mind their own business. But over and over again, the ordinary village folk are the victims of this terrible war. They are the grass that is trampled upon when the big elephants fight. Again and again they have to find an accommodation with whichever victorious warlord happens to cross their path.

When we return to the tent, the people of Lafon are called together. All along they have followed the proceedings at a distance. Chairs and a few benches from a neighbouring school are carried over to provide proper seating for the guests. Again we are welcomed by Commander William as friends of Sudan. 'If you want to know whether you have any friends, all you have to do is fall ill and your real friends will come and visit you. Southern Sudan is gangrenous with the evil of war, and you have come to visit us. You indeed must be real friends.' There is loud applause. Is this man really our opponent, I wonder? Then I remember that so far not a word has been said about Joseph Okello, the object of our mission! Bishop Taban rises and thanks everyone for the warm welcome. He tells us that peace has to grow in the hearts of the people themselves; it cannot be engineered from without. He asks the Important Guest (I am numbered among them) if we have any peace for export in Germany, Norway, Belgium, Holland? No? Then he speaks about making peace with others. Yes, over and over again things tend to go wrong, especially between people of quality. That's what has happened here in Lafon. Would anyone deny that Commander William Nyoun is a man of high calibre? No, none of us would deny it. He continues: 'We, here in Lafon, are pleased to have a church leader who is also of great standing. His name is Father Joseph Okello.' This is the first time since we arrived in Lafon that his name is mentioned. The bishop explains how important it is for great leaders to talk together and that they have much to say to one another. And he tells the people what has been happening over the past few weeks. 'Joseph has been in the base camp of William Nyoun where they have straightened out their differences. He has returned to Lafon this morning. In fact, here he is.'

And then suddenly, Joseph Okello appears out of nowhere. The people applaud enthusiastically while he embraces the bishop and greets the commander and the visitors. He greets the people and says that he is happy to be back in Lafon. He takes a seat between Paride and me. Whilst the people sing a song he takes the opportunity to talk to the bishop. Yes, it is true that he was arrested and held for several weeks by William Nyoun. He had been afraid he might be handed over to the government. He is hugely relieved that we have come to free him. We all feel that we have liberated Joseph and we expect him to fly with us to Nairobi.

However, to my surprise, the bishop asks Joseph to stay on for another week. If he would come with us now the impression would be given that William was forced to let him go. Then it would look as if we would have won and William would appear to be the loser. The bishop promises that he will send another priest in a week's time to take Joseph's place. I find this a tall order for Joseph, but he understands, especially when he hears that in Nairobi scores of journalists are waiting to interview him. He has no clothes but what he is wearing. He washed them this morning and they were drying in the sun when we arrived. A Belgian of comparable size and frame offers him a T-shirt and pair of trousers.

Now it is time to celebrate; the bull has been slaughtered, and there are rice and vegetables brought by the Norwegians. Commander William Nyoun sits at the head of the table flanked by Bishop Taban and Joseph Okello. I observe them from some distance and it suddenly strikes me that this is not show: they really enjoy one another's company whilst they recall events of the past. It is as if the mistake of arresting Joseph Okello does not take away all the good that this Commander William also has done.

An hour or so later, we are at the airstrip in the scorching heat of the afternoon sun. William Nyoun and his soldiers, with Joseph Okello and his parishioners, see us off. Commander William carries a young antelope caught by one of his soldiers. He offers it to Bishop Paride as a farewell present. The bishop has to refuse because there is a ban on importing animals into Kenya, but it would be impolite to refuse out of hand. So the bishop accepts the little animal, and gives it to Joseph to care for in Lafon.

We climb into the plane and when we take off, we can see Joseph and William standing side by side waving at us. As the hills of Lafon recede below, Bishop Paride thanks us for having been such 'friendly guests'. For our part we are relieved that everything went so smoothly, and we all feel a little less confident in our own notions of diplomacy, a little less smug. Then the bishop leans back in his seat and falls asleep. It is not his way to talk about loving your enemy; that is not African; he simply refuses to see a fellow human as an enemy; that is more African.

A week later, I meet Joseph Okello in Nairobi. He is relieved to be out of the maelstrom, and says with a faint , smile, 'Our friend William sends you his greetings'. It is a few years since all this happened. Joseph Okello now works as a missionary in South Africa and Commander William Nyoun was killed in the war. The bullet that killed him may well have been fired from a gun held by a government soldier, as Bishop Taban had hinted in the story he told at Lafon. The forgotten war continues, well beyond the glaring lights of the international media. The government in Khartoum still plays fast and loose with human rights with impunity: the systematic genocide of the inhabitants of the Nuba Mountains is well documented. Forced Islamization and the imposition of Shari'a law make a mockery of the rights of minorities. The SPLA is not without blame either. Children are rounded up in recruitment drives for the rebel army. NGOs are coerced into providing food for the soldiers. Like any war, this is a dirty war. But what right do we have to point an accusing finger at the Sudanese if we do not ask where those bombs, grenades and land mines come from? Is there no way of breaking out of this infernal circle?

THE FLIES AND THE BEES

Fire cannot be extinguished with fire.
Kikuyu proverb

Together with some Sudanese friends I am sitting in the
dark under the beautiful star spangled sky in Yambio
(southern Sudan). It is quiet; the sounds of the African
evening, the crickets and the muffled beat of drums in the
distance belong to that silence. We drink freshly-made
orange juice; oranges are ripe at this time. I have tried to
tell my friends how I fared since we sat here together last
year. I remember it was the time of the mango harvest and
that we were eating them together. There is something
peaceful about the evening and my friends, too, radiate a
certain calmness and contentment. The recent harvest
was good: without much outside help they had even been
able to feed the more than 50,000 refugees who had
returned from Congo. Sudan now seems a safer place
than Congo. Those refugees have begun to set up their
own gardens. Shortly the hospital in Yambio will start its
activities again. It all sounds very hopeful, even though
the rays of light are not as many as the stars.

Suddenly there is the sound of gunshots and people
screaming. Frightened, we listen to that cruel disturbance
of the calmness. Father Justin gets up and goes towards
the noise. The screaming stops. We only hear a man carrying on a bit. Some ten minutes later a gun is fired empty.
Uncertain we stand together, not knowing what to do.
Fortunately Justin soon returns. A drunken Dinka soldier,
not hailing from this area, had fired at a few people.

Thank God no one was hit! Justin tells us he had hidden behind a tree, had tried to strike up a conversation with the gunman and had asked him to hand over the gun. The drunken soldier refused but eventually emptied the gun, firing into the air. Then he had been taken home by some bystanders. In the nick of time a minor tribal war had been prevented. There is not much left of our peaceful evening.

The incident loosens up the tongues. Instead of positive stories I am now told how many things keep going wrong. People fulminate at soldiers of other tribes, even though it is just as often soldiers of the local tribe who have deserted who make the neighbourhood unsafe. The situation in Sudan has not improved much since my visit last year. As a result of the good harvest and the cease-fire proclaimed by the government to allow the aid organizations the opportunity to take food to the victims of hunger in Bahr el Ghazal, there are not many deaths from starvation at this moment, but the next hunger period is already very near. But the cease-fire does not imply that the government has stopped bombing civilian targets: even the hospital at Yei was bombed three times. Angry and gloomy, my friends wonder when it will be Yambio's turn to get hit again. Some of them want anti-aircraft guns; the tone of the conversation turns aggressive. I am told of the rumour that the government uses the cease-fire to regroup its troops and provide them with arms. Why does the international community not do anything? Why do they only make a move when dying babies are shown on television? Their reproach implies fear and powerlessness. Will it never stop? Is the situation really hopeless? On the one hand there is a conference going on to bring about peace between the Nuer and the Dinka, and at the same time a small war has started again between the SPLA and the local Didinga. The soldiers, too, are fed up with the long war without payment; some have become common robbers.

I hear that Bishop Paride Taban is trying to mediate in the latest clash in his diocese. He went into the mountains to talk to the local people who had sought refuge there, and accompanied by a few leaders he came down to discuss matters with the SPLA. Some in my company think he is too soft: he ought to take a more assertive stance by pressing charges against these abuses.

A few days later I have a talk with the bishop in Lokichokio. He is here for the annual diocesan meeting. It was decided to hold the meeting here in Kenya because the presence of so many cars in Sudan might provoke an aerial bombardment. Paride Taban has great hopes that the conflict between the local population and the SPLA will soon be settled. He talks about his plans to gather a group of people from the educational sector and health services and to train them in trauma counselling. Children have been traumatized by the war, and the mothers too have suffered serious emotional damage. The children, but also the mothers, should be helped in coming to terms with their traumatic experiences. Peace must begin from below, says Paride Taban; people must be taught to keep the peace with themselves and with each other. He tells me about the many problems in his diocese, but nevertheless keeps a positive view of things. I ask him if he is being realistic. After all, he too knows all the negative stories that I have heard these last few days. Surely he will not deny that they are true. Tomorrow he has to address the people working in his diocese. Is he going to tell them things are not so bad after all, and that all is well with Sudan?

No, he has no intention to say that all is well. But he is not quite sure yet what he does want to tell. He has been thinking about it, though. 'No man is wise by himself', he says. 'It is good to share one's ideas with someone else. By discussing them with others one can sharpen them somewhat'. Whilst thinking aloud about his speech for tomorrow he asks me to be his whetstone.

'Look' he says, 'people are often like flies: they look for dirt, and the more refuse has been collected the happier they seem to be. They fly from one pile of dung to the other. That is how they spread disease and infirmity and foul up the entire community. Some people become blind, others deaf or fall victim to another illness. Thus people may even cause each other's death. If no one warns them they might even go after a corpse being taken away for burial. They might be buried together with that corpse.'

Now there are people who want to make a clean sweep of all those flies. Not an easy thing to do! I remember going for a picnic once with a group of youngsters years ago. While walking through the forest we came to an open space and one lad said: 'Look, what a nice open spot! We can picnic and even camp here. Come and have a look, there is not a single fly about. It is the nicest place you can imagine.' However another boy said: 'That may well be so, but we will have to relieve ourselves somewhere and you bet there will be flies then'.

Paride Taban cannot hide a faint smile at this thought. He is too much of an African not to know there is no world without flies. Of course, one must try to keep one's house and surroundings clean to limit the number of flies as much as possible, but they will always keep coming.

Then he continues his story.

'Fortunately there are not only flies, there are also bees. Do I know how bees live?' he wonders. I tell him that to me bees are a symbol of hard work, the busy bee. That sounds quite reasonable to him. He is not against hard work, but it is not the first thing that comes to his mind when he thinks about bees. 'Bees are quite different from flies', he says. 'In fact bees only look for what is good for themselves, nectar and pollen. You might even call them selfish. But the beautiful thing about it is that they do not keep it to themselves only, it is for the benefit of the entire colony. They even show each other the way to the tasty nectar in the flowers. Together they collect sufficient to feed on, not only then, but they also make provisions for the time when flowers are hard to find. In Sudan we are now in the dry season: there are not many flowers now. Still, there will be a time when they blossom forth again and the bees will perform their special job then. That special job does not only consist of collecting nectar. More important may well be that during their activities they carry the pollen from one flower to the other. Thus the bees pollinate the plants and the trees, which in their turn can bear fruit.'

He looks at me to see if I have anything to add to this. No, I have nothing to add. The choice is ours: are we going to work like flies or bees! That is the question he will put to his people tomorrow.

I have promised him to put this question also to my own people. When we sat there together silently for a moment, I dared to think again that peace is possible.

SUDAN: THE BACKGROUND

It is not easy to find reliable figures about Sudan: the country is so big and diverse, and often people supply the numbers which they consider most advantageous to their particular situation. I would not swear that the following is correct, but I think it comes close.

AREA: Sudan occupies 966,757 square miles, more than one quarter the area of the USA. A great part is desert and infertile, but 12%, along the Nile and in parts of the south, is good agricultural land. In 1990 it was estimated that 18% of the country was forest. Parts of the south are semi-rainforest and are very fertile indeed.

POPULATION: The population of Sudan is estimated at about 25 million, of whom about 5 million have been displaced in the civil war which has continued in one guise or another since independence in 1956. Of the 25 million about 4.5 million used to live in the south of Sudan. Nearly half the Sudanese are ethnically Arabs, and half belong ethnically to African tribes, of which the Dinka is the largest.

LANGUAGES: Arabic is the official language, certainly in the north. In the south English is also spoken, alongside more than 100 tribal languages. It is said that about 25 of these languages are each spoken by more than 100,000 people.

GOVERNMENT: Sudan is at present a republic with single-party military rule. The government is solidly in the hands of the National Islamic Front which favours an Islamic fundamentalism, imposing Shari'a law.

ECONOMY: The main source of income for Sudan is agriculture, especially in parts of the fertile south. Another source of income could be oil, which has been discovered in the neighbourhood of Bentiu. The present conflict has ruined the economy, and Sudan has become one of the poorest countries in Africa. Military expenses of the government in 1994 were nearly 300 million US dollars in 1994. Inflation runs at over 40% a year.

RELIGION: 70% of the population is Muslim, 10% follow traditional African religions, and 20% belong to various Christian denominations, which are growing very fast at present.

LIFE EXPECTANCY: The life expectancy of people in Sudan is estimated at 48 years, but in the south of Sudan it is much lower. 118 infants of every thousand die. It is estimated that nearly 1.5 million people, mainly southerners, have died as a result of the civil war.

LITERACY: No exact figures are available, but in the south education has practically come to a standstill because of the war. The estimate of literacy for men is 30–35% and for women about 15%.[1]

---

[1]One source for some of these figures is *The Human Development Report*, 1996.

SUDAN AND ITS WARS

The poor man and the rich man do not play together
Ashanti proverb

Sudan, 'The Land of Dark People', is what the Arabs named this land long ago. But until today less dark people have tried to claim and hold it. The Egyptian Pharaohs saw it as a possible grain silo for their country. As early as 2800 BC, Egypt occupied Nubia, which is now part of North Sudan. The country has always been important to Egypt, since the White and the Blue Nile which flow through Sudan are tributaries to their Nile.

It is an old country, older than the Bible. Many southern Sudanese will tell you that their country is referred to in the Old Testament: in Isaiah 18, there is mention of a people, tall and smooth-skinned, a people feared near and far, a nation mighty and conquering, whose land rivers divide. Often the present-day inhabitants associate themselves with the suffering people of the Old Testament. They feel that through the centuries they have been enslaved as Israel was enslaved. When Africa was for Europeans still a great dark continent, the Arabs were getting their slaves and ivory from Sudan. The anti-Arabic sentiments in the south go back to the time of the slave trade.

As early as the fourteenth century, the entire area between the Blue Nile and the White Nile was under Arab influence. At the beginning of the nineteenth century, Egypt conquered the present Sudan.

In 1881 the Sheik of Dongola, the great Al-Mahdi,

succeeded in regaining Sudanese independence, but it did not last very long. The white man grew interested in the Land of the Dark People: England lent Egypt a helping hand in reoccupying Sudan, and in 1889 Sudan came under British rule. It remained in the hands of Great Britain for more than fifty years.

These days, Sudan is the largest country in Africa, almost one million square miles, that is one-quarter of the size of the USA. One can hardly say that it is densely populated, with 25 million inhabitants, of whom two million live in the capital, Khartoum. Great tracts of the country are desolate; the north is largely desert with fertile strips only along the Nile. Here the population is mainly Arabic. Over 430 miles south of Khartoum the large swamps begin, formed by the White Nile with its many tributaries. These swamps, called the Sudd, are the largest swamplands in the world. They form a natural border between the north and south of Sudan.

Many tribes have their homes here in the south: the Dinka, the Nuer, and the Azande are probably the best known. Because of their isolation, for many centuries they went unnoticed by the outside world. One cannot say that the British colonized them to the extent that they did other people. There was little glory in colonizing this territory. Visiting it as an explorer, Baker said, 'Everything was wild and cruel, hard and insensitive. This caused a fundamental uncertainty among all whites penetrating into southern Sudan, a feeling of being in a wilderness where life never progressed, but just went on in a timeless and aimless circle.'[1] Even these days, I meet people who think as Baker did 160 years ago.

For the most part, the English kept the people in the south outside the sphere of Arab influence. They were fodder for anthropologists and missionaries. It was probably the missionaries who were the strongest influence from the outside world. Colonial administration was minimal, and often more linked to the administration in Uganda than the administration in the north of Sudan.

---

[1]Alan Moorehead, *The White Nile*, New York, Dell Publishing Co., 1960, p.95.

Education was very much left to the Protestant and Catholic missions, each church being given its own territory to evangelize. The great missionary Daniel Comboni, and his followers, the Comboni Missionaries, have probably contributed most, especially in the field of education. My colleagues, the Mill Hill Missionaries, are still working in Upper Nile, around Malakal.

The north and the south of Sudan were joined together when Sudan became independent in 1956, and since then there has been little peace in the land. It is not easy to understand this long war, but it is a little easier if we know some of the historical background.

What is called Sudan today has never been one country for any length of time. It was united for the first time under Turko-Egyptian domination from 1820–1. It is important to remember that it was not united under British colonial rule. Realizing, after trying to end slavery, that they could not simply unite those who were once slavemasters and slaves, the British kept the north and the south separate under a system of indirect rule. They administered the south from Uganda and the north via Egypt.

It was partly at the request of Egypt that North and South Sudan were united before independence in 1956. Since then many governments have fallen before their time, usually because they were not able to solve what was dubbed 'The Southern Problem'. Many battles have been fought by the various governments against the south of Sudan. Many lives have been lost, and the most tragic part is that the governments usually used soldiers from the south to fight the southern freedom fighters.

The first civil war between the north and the south started before independence. Later on it came to be called *Anya-nya*. It was about the political and economic domination by the north, and religious disunity played a role. The government operated a policy of 'divide and rule', which was easy, given the great ethnic diversity of the south. When a southern leader, Joseph Lagu, managed to unite the different rebel movements, Colonel Numeiri, who came to power in Khartoum in 1969, had to choose a path of reconciliation, which, with the help of the churches, resulted in the Addis Ababa agreement. This was the beginning of about ten years of relative peace. There were plans for big development in the south, but they were not always designed to benefit the people there. Oil was discovered in Bentiu, and the north was inclined to redraw the boundaries so that Bentiu would belong to the north. Another massive development project that got under way was the digging of the Jonglei Canal, to drain the great Sudd. But the ulterior motive was that the canal would provide more water for the north and Egypt. When Numeiri introduced the Islamic Shari'a laws in 1983, it was more than the southerners could take. It was the beginning of a new civil war, this time led by the Dinka. Dr John Garang became the leader of the new liberation movement called the SPLA (Sudan People's Liberation Army).

In 1986, President Sadiq al-Mahdi came to power, leading a coalition government, which after some time came to include the National Islamic Front (NIF). The NIF is an Islamic fundamentalist organization whose main objective in the government was the issuing of the Shari'a laws. When Sadiq al-Mahdi and the SPLA achieved a measure of entente in 1989, the leader of the NIF, Hassan al-Turabi, instigated a successful military coup. Under this military government, Arabization and Islamization increased, and life for the people of black African descent became very difficult. The south lost much; even Juba University, the only university in the south of Sudan, was closed.

Then began the systematic eradication of the Nuba people who, though Moslem, are in many ways support- ive of the SPLA. The government wants to use the extensive fertile grazing ground in the Nuba mountains for extensive cattle breeding. The people of the Nuba mountain are the victims of this policy. Villages are eradi- cated and the people are placed in the so called 'peace-camps' where often they are forced to become Moslems. In that way the government tries to break the opposition. Culture, religion and struggle for control over the land all play a role in the war against the Nuba people.

At first the SPLA made steady progress in the armed conflict, but this all changed in 1991 when it split into two factions. As in the past, the government exploited the disunity in the south and soon there was further fragmentation of the rebels. The SPLA lost ground for its cause when it was accused of human rights violations, one of them being that they forced children to become soldiers. War-torn Sudan has had, in its forty years of independence, hardly ten years of peace. War crimes and human rights violations continue. More than three-quarters of the people in South Sudan have become displaced within their own country, or are refugees in neighbouring countries. Almost the entire infrastructure in the south has been destroyed. It is beyond the imagination to understand that in an area twenty-five times the size of Holland, there is hardly a shop left, no petrol station that works, no proper education system, no money economy. Still the people survive, largely because they evidence a strong sense of community.

Several times, neighbouring countries have tried to intervene and broker peace, especially Kenya, Uganda, Ethiopia and Eritrea, which are united with Sudan in IGADD (Intergovernmental Authority on Drought and Development). Also from within the Sudan people have taken peace initiatives, supported by the churches. But all these efforts have been to no avail.

It is a complicated war and it is important to remember that not only Sudanese parties play a role in this war. Of course, other nations are involved in the struggle. Fundamentalist Islamic regimes support the Khartoum government, and supply it with weapons and occasionally with soldiers. The UN Security Council has threatened the Sudan government with sanctions several times, holding it responsible for supporting terrorism and harbouring terrorists. It is generally accepted that the United States of America has been covertly supplying the neighbouring countries of Sudan with military support, vicariously providing assistance to the SPLA. But somehow the National Islamic Front, led by Hassan al-Turabi, remains in control, and it is very often underestimated by the world community.

The war cannot any longer be called a war between the north and south. The opposition in the north, the National Democratic Alliance (NDA) has started to join together with the SPLA. In 1997, the SPLA and the NDA fought together against the government troops in Blue Nile province. The SPLA regained a lot of terrain along the border of Uganda and the NDA attacked several positions of the government in North Sudan in the area of Port Sudan. Although the NDA is recognized internationally as an important political factor, the government of Sudan remains opposed to its participation in the IGADD peace negotiations. At present the government tries to recruit young students for the Jihad, holy war, against the Christians.

It is quite clear that religious conflict is not the origin of this war. But as the war continues the original causes become more and more obscured, and religion seems to play a more important role. That is the reason why these days this war is often described as a 'religious war'. That is also why the peace process again and again bogs down over principles of the 'secular state' and 'self-determination'. It is very much a question whether this war will ever end as long as the Shari'a laws remain in place.

At present there seems to be no solution in sight. In the end, only the people of Sudan can resolve the conflict.

EPILOGUE

I don't know who Jean Dodo is and I don't know where he comes from, but I found this poem written by him among papers of a missionary in Chicago. We talk about mission as dialogue and we develop new theories and we try to understand each other, but it all becomes meaningful only when we truly meet each other, as Jean Dodo explains in his poem.

That evening on the beach far away,
we spoke no broken French,
whilst eating roasted sweet bananas.

We used old and wise words,
words older than both of us,
words full of life and images.

He spoke to me about his mother;
his is white, mine is black,
but they love in the same way.

I spoke to him about my village:
his is built of brick, mine of grass,
but the ancestors have the same silences.

He told me about his youth
and we both hope we will meet there again.
He played in the snow and I in the sand.

I spoke to him about sorrow and pain.
He knows them well and I no less,
but we both have the same tears to heal them.

I spoke to him about life hereafter.
There is sunshine in his, water in mine
and we hope to meet there again.

The night heard and understood our words.
On the beach of old wisdom,
there is still the light of our eyes and the gold
of the bananas.

Jean Dodo